{noise}

{noise}

Joseph McCormack

{noise}

**living and leading when
nobody can focus ◄**

WILEY

Library of Congress Cataloging-in-Publication Data is Available:

ISBN 9781394324262 (Paperback)
ISBN 9781119553373 (Cloth)
ISBN 9781119553366 (ePub)
ISBN 9781119553359 (ePDF)

Cover Design: Megan Palicki
Cover Image: © pingebat / Shutterstock
Author Photo: courtesy of the Author

SKY10086913_100424

This book is dedicated to all of my brothers and sisters (Mary Carol, Jean, Matt, Peg, Annie, Kate, John, and Patrick), a constant source of encouragement, laughter, inspiration, and love. From my childhood to the present day, they are the best family one could have. In particular, I dedicate this book to my late brother Johnny, my best friend and closest collaborator, whom I miss dearly every day and work hard to honor.

CONTENTS

Part **ONE**

WEAPONS OF MASS DISTRACTION   1

1 *Noise, Noise, So Much Noise*   *3*

Kenny Chesney Gets It Right
Hearing Decline and the Loss of Focus
Access to Information Will Only Increase
Attention Spans Will Remain Elusive
Our Minds Will Become Anemic and Impenetrable

2 *Huh? We're Going Collectively Deaf*   *11*

So, Why Do We Tune Out? A Variety of Reasons
The Impact of the "Elusive 600" on Our Listening
How Words Become Worthless—and Triggers for a Tune-Out
My Mom Thought I Had a Hearing Problem

Part **TWO**

THE BIG TUNE-OUT IS COMING (IMAGINING THE UNTHINKABLE—SIX SHORT STORIES TO WAKE YOU UP) 41

10 *Safety Briefing with Near-Tragic Results*   *85*

Part THREE

TIME FOR YOU TO TUNE IN: AWARENESS
MANAGEMENT (AM 101)   *93*

11 *Awareness Management 101*   *95*

Lighting the Path Before Us
Lives Can Become a Blur
Missing the Moment Entirely
Our Minds Are Spinning Beach Balls
The Elusive 600: Your Enemy or Your Friend?
Runaway Thoughts
Waking Your Mind from Mindlessness to Mindfulness
Directed, Undirected, and Misdirected
Commit to "Awareness Management"
What If We Don't Manage Our Awareness?
AM Pre-set Buttons

12 *Take Aim: Set Your Sights on What Matters Most*   *109*

Essentialists versus Non-essentialists
No More Deafening Noise
Pointless Routines
A Minimalist Decision: Keep It Simple
Aim Small, Miss Small—Tips to Direct Your Focus
Post It: Simplicity Isn't Complicated
To Simplify Is a Deliberate Decision

Part **FOUR**

Part **FIVE**

PRE-SETS: SIMPLE PROGRAMMING FOR
NOISE REDUCTION   215

FOREWORD

Joe graciously mailed me a pre-release copy of *NOISE*, the book you're now holding. After reading it, I conducted a little experiment:

I disabled my e-mail alerts, shushed my social, and nuked (most of) my notifications.

Muzzled. Gag-ordered. Zipped.

Mind you, I didn't delete any of my accounts. I've in no way pulled a Henry David Thoreau and left the digital city for the analog woods altogether. This is neither a "Finished with Facebook!" freakout, nor a "malaise of modernity" manifesto. Rather:

I simply realized I was done with being *distracted*.

Field Notes from Three Months in a Quiet Place:

- Once you get below a certain threshold of "omnipresent sound and fury," you start to take more notice of those few distractions that *do* sneak through. Like a single person gabbing in a library, you *hear* them more intensely than any single, screaming voice in a crowd. Case in point: I found myself wondering, "Is it in *any* way acceptable that *Yahoo! Sports* is daring to bother me about Florida Atlantic Football Coach Lane Kiffin right now? On a Tuesday morning? This is a library!" So, I turned off those notifications, too.

- You start to develop a calming, confidence-building sense of flow and control. You begin … [*Scout's Honor: As I sit here writing this, my Apple Watch taps me on the wrist to let me know that Americans eat 554 million Jack in the Box tacos a year, and no one knows why. Sorry WSJ ... You're now shushed too.*] Nuts! I lost my train of thought. What was I saying? Oh yes: You begin to realize that context-switching is a productivity killer, and that every time you're dragged off course by an unexpected distraction, you've just lost real time and money. Your mind takes time to accelerate into whatever it is you're focusing on next. Too many "nexts," and you're forever stuck in first gear.

- My various digital *assistants* had become my digital *bosses*. By constantly demanding my attention, my phone had pulled rank and began to call the shots. I'd really like to finish this Foreword right now, but *bossypants* has swooped in and demanded that I focus on tacos. By simply resetting my relationship with my devices to *pull* as opposed to *push*, I find that they're profoundly less ... pushy. Suddenly, my phone is back to taking orders as the trusty personal assistant I'd originally "hired" way back in 2007.

This important book, *NOISE*, is ultimately about Attention Economics. About the idea that a "wealth of information creates a poverty of attention, and a need to allocate that attention efficiently among the overabundance of information sources that might consume it."

Nobel Prize–winning economist Herbert Simon wrote that quoted bit in 1971. Before smartphones. Before the Web. Before cable TV.

Nearly 50 years on, Joe McCormack brings us the means to prosper in this "poverty." *NOISE* isn't a radical license to unplug and live in an uninformed bubble, but a playbook to help us be radically intentional about the sources—and formats—of information worthy of our precious time and attention. Not earplugs: a hearing aid.

Consider *NOISE* both a challenge and an encouragement to attend to your plan—not the next "ding."

—Mike Bechtel
Futurist, Deloitte
Professor of Corporate Innovation, University of Notre Dame

Addendum

Moving beyond digital interventions, I've since posted a paper sign outside my home office door that says: "Dad's Busy Earning Your Roof, Meals, & Allowance. Emergencies Only!"

I hear racing footfalls of my 7- and 9-year-olds, building to a crescendo.

Knock Knock Knock.

"Dad's working, guys. Is it an emergency?"

"Yes. Well ... kind of."

"Okay. What's up?"

They proceed to throw open the door to notify me that a new season of *Stranger Things* has just dropped.

Unable to shush my children, I consider disabling Netflix.

PREFACE

Can you stop the flood?

Your best bet is to get out of the way or find a boat to float to safety. We are in an unnerving moment in history: information is becoming more of a threat than a reward.

You can't get out of its way, so how do you handle all of it and not have it overwhelm you?

When I wrote *BRIEF: Make a bigger impact by saying less* in 2013, my biggest concern was helping people learn to be clear and concise. Basically, get your point across or get dismissed.

Dedicating myself the past few years to spreading the message that "less is more," I am alarmed by a growing trend that the need for brevity reveals: information is so readily accessible that it is now burdening us.

It all sounds like senseless noise.

Focus is a huge problem. People's attention spans are shrinking, and it's no joke. It's harder and harder to tune in to the essentials and tune out what drowns us.

There are two sides to the coin.

Certainly, one side of the issue is brevity—cutting through the clutter. Essentially, think of it as an adaptive strategy: get to the point before someone tunes you out.

Yet, the other side is how to avoid tuning into nonstop static in an always-on, connected life. How can we stay mentally focused when faced with such information inundation?

As I start seeing progress on one side of the issue, developing lean communicators and setting a higher communication standard, I feel there's also a larger battle we are losing.

The point of this book is to set off an alarm: the world is going deaf. We've gone far beyond the promise of the information age and are now so consumed by it that it threatens our existence.

Here's a dire picture of our world moving forward:

- Managers don't know how to talk to their subordinates.
- Leaders cannot rally their distracted followers.
- Spouses talk past each other, and relationships suffer.
- Children constantly tune out their parents.
- Parents can't listen to their kids.
- Fans follow sports but don't really watch the games.
- Sales professionals don't comprehend what their customers really need.
- Civil discourse is lost in senseless arguments and pointless persuasion.
- Days are wasted consuming empty brain calories.
- Progress, insight, and learning stall.
- We all grow apart.

Our lives in an information age are like facing a tsunami. Being able to hold onto something sturdy, permanent, and solid means a chance to survive and thrive. Giving into the endless sources of distraction and empty information means getting swept permanently out to sea.

The threat of infobesity is profound and potentially permanent for generations to come.

What matters most to me is helping people get better at surviving this calamity. I've spent so much time over the past few years witnessing a deep erosion of focus that I'm motivated to help those willing, interested, and able to withstand the societal shift that threatens our ability to communicate and connect with each other.

We need to maintain what makes us really human.

Our focus as a society is dwindling as our addiction to screens, technology, distractions, and interruptions grows. We're becoming mentally anemic, consuming useless information with little value.

This is an enormous issue that will forever change our lives. Will the implications of incessant information consumption make us all collectively deaf to one another?

This was my motivation writing this book. How can we adapt when getting drowned out in so much noise in all facets of our lives?

It's time for noise abatement.

{noise}

HOW THE BOOK IS ORGANIZED

PART	I	II	III	IV	V
QUESTION	WHY?	WHY WORRY?	HOW DO WE IMPROVE?	HOW CAN WE HELP OTHERS?	WHAT'S NEXT?
TITLE	Weapons of Mass Distraction	The Big Tune-Out Is Coming	Awareness Management (AM 101)	Focus Management (FM 101)	Pre-Sets: Simple Programming for Noise Reduction
IN SIX WORDS	Noise, noise, always so much noise	Short stories to wake you up	Be aware of your own awareness	Get others to tighten their focus	Practical daily challenges to dial in
THE GIST	Our brains are being barraged and it is seriously affecting a broad spectrum of society	Each of us feels the impact of information overload in very personal and permanent ways	It is a personal responsibility to manage how and when we choose to control our attention	We can help others around us by taking practical steps that will make them feel quick relief	Like you dial into a radio by pre-programming stations, these challenges quickly get you ready to focus
YOUR FEELING	Curious		Captivated		Committed
BOTTOM LINE	The more information we consume, the less we retain	Infobesity is a serious societal shift that we must address	There are simple things we can do to regain our brains	We can influence how others improve their focus	We can drown out noise with clarity and control

HOW TO READ THIS BOOK

NOISE is designed to make it easier for you to maintain focus while reading the book. Intentionally, I have included periodic breaks to allow you to go deeper on a thought or take a short break with a brief insight. Here is what's inside for you:

SOUNDBITES:
These simple insights remind us how to protect ourselves from more noise and concentrate more intentionally. They are short and sweet suggestions meant to produce clarity, focus, peace, and calm.

NOTEWORTHY:
These are full-page features that shed light on noise abatement, whether it's about an innovative person, a published work, or a key idea to improve attention. In each case, I make it clear why it's worth our careful consideration.

NOISE MAKERS:
Throughout the book, I have included a series of illustrations that help capture not only what causes so many distractions and so much inattention, but also where that impact is felt throughout our daily lives.

ACKNOWLEDGMENTS

The title of this book is a story unto itself.

For several months, the initial project operated under the working title *In One Ear, and Out the Other.* Though catchy, it didn't completely capture and communicate the true essence of the book's message. One day, I had a brainstorm session with my close collaborators, project manager Ania Waz and editor Karen Quinn, in my office in suburban Chicago.

Through that clarifying conversation, *NOISE* emerged. I cannot thank both of them enough for their untiring commitment from beginning to end on this journey.

Excited and energized with the new title, I started spreading the word to my co-workers, collaborators, and close friends. For a year, the vision got clearer, and people's enthusiastic reactions motivated me onward. In particular, my siblings never stop encouraging me, specifically my sisters Peggy and Ann, and my brother Matt—all of my family, for that matter.

I've always seen this book as a companion to *BRIEF* and, in some ways, even a prequel. Designing the cover, I knew the two titles needed to look like alike—almost siblings—paired and meant to be read together since their content goes hand in hand. I cannot thank enough Megan Palicki and Joan Bueta, two talented designers, who also helped me with the first book and for whom I have the highest admiration for their creativity, taste, and strong brand sense. They didn't disappoint and brought the vision to life, not only with the cover but also with their many illustrations. Thanks again for being there for me and staying part of the family.

I also counted on a number of individuals for ongoing support in writing this book. First off, Brian Neill and Vicki Adang at John Wiley & Sons. Also, Joyce Duriga, Marc McCormack, and Mickey Novak, with research and editing.

My co-workers continue to believe in me and my vision. In particular, I need to thank Charley Thornton and our team in Chicago who lead our corporate practice. As for my Southern Pines, North Carolina, team, I appreciate the constant support and fun-loving spirit of Michelle McKinney, Steve Cain, and Jill Catron, who encourage and affirm me day to day as we serve our military clients.

Finally, I need to thank my clients, both present and past, for taking on our challenge and asking us to do even more for them. Setting an elite communication standard is only a viable vision if there are people, teams, and organizations with the commitment, courage, and discipline to embrace it every day. Thanks for stepping up and setting the tone.

Part One

Weapons of Mass Distraction

Part One

1 Noise, Noise, So Much Noise

> To the hard of hearing, you shout.
> —*Flannery O'Connor*

We're all connected, all day and in every way. Smartphones, laptops, tablets, and smart watches. Screens in cars, airports, gas stations, classrooms, offices, hospitals, and hotels. The constant buzzing of a 24-hour news cycle. The list goes on.

What? Did you just miss that? Maybe you got another text, news alert, or notification?

The daily experience is to consume information at every turn. It's nearly impossible to avoid the barrage from morning until night. How much of it is relevant? What's useful for us, and what is simply a waste of time and energy?

Our brains are hard at work, making it harder to focus and easier than ever to get distracted. Our attention spans are rapidly eroding, and we're now at risk. Over the years, we adapt. Many of us don't even notice this decline because we're too busy fixating on the next distraction, text message, e-mail, meeting invitation, social media post, or funny video clip.

Infobesity is the new normal, and it can have dire consequences. Here's a snapshot of where we consume information:

- **Overflowing e-mail.** Our inboxes are flooded with messages; most of them are irrelevant and yet they keep coming over and over to be read, judged useless, and then deleted.

- **Smartphone notifications.** Throughout the day, our phones vibrate and sound the alarm to be picked up and checked.

- **Checking our devices.** For most of us, it's the first and last thing we do every day.

- **Social media streams.** We fear missing out on the latest posts and updates and try to keep up on the steady stream of commentary and tidbits being shared every few seconds by our personal and professional networks.

- **24-hour connectivity.** While we sleep, the flow of information doesn't stop and can be consumed on every imaginable device, at any time.

- **Texting and messaging.** Immediate ways to communicate that we can't seem to resist sending or receiving.

- **News feed frenzy.** A story breaks and unleashes the frenetic obsession to cover, repeat, recycle, rehash, argue, and opine until the content and audience are left exhausted.

- **Time spent online.** The amount of time online exceeds offline in the age of information overload and constant consumption.

All of this feels like nonstop, won't-stop noise.

There's a serious impact when we expose ourselves to these alarming conditions all day long. In a life with always-on access to information, we now face a shrinking, elusive attention span and an overstimulated, overfilled brain.

What can we do to adapt and manage this new reality?

Kenny Chesney Gets It Right

The country singer Kenny Chesney laments this common condition wonderfully in his song "Noise." His lyrics tell the story of how our society has taken a turn for the worse, with so much noise surrounding us that there is no room for silence. We don't ask for it, but we're bombarded with constant chatter from talking heads and distractions from digital devices, and we can't escape it anymore.

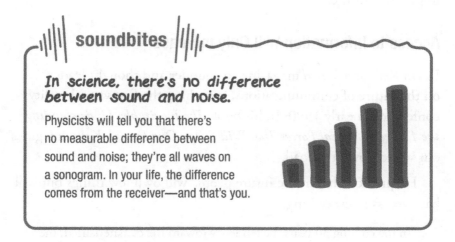

soundbites

In science, there's no different between sound and noise.

Physicists will tell you that there's no measurable difference between sound and noise; they're all waves on a sonogram. In your life, the difference comes from the receiver—and that's you.

Hearing Decline and the Loss of Focus

When I was in college in Chicago, I remember an elderly Jesuit philosophy professor opening every lecture with an impassioned, personal, public service announcement. He would warn us of the impending threat of loud music on our hearing. It was in the late 1980s, and boomboxes and rock concerts were all the rage, along with the advent of portable music devices like the Sony Walkman. His dire concern, backed by extensive research, was that too much loud music would make us all deaf.

And once that happened, he said sternly, we wouldn't be able to fix the permanent hearing loss.

Sorry.

There is a close connection between hearing loss and declining focus. You have loud music and volume levels and constant information and attention spans. You have listening capacity and mental retention. Noise affects our ability to hear; information overload affects our ability to pay attention.

It's the perfect storm. Let's take a look at how these things will impact our future.

Access to Information Will Only Increase

Kevin Kelly is a *Wired* magazine co-founder and thought leader on the future of communications, launching the first virtual reality conference in early 1990. In his book *The Inevitable: Understanding the 12 Technological Forces That Will Shape Our Future,* Kelly imagines our world down the road.

He predicts that in the future people will own few things but will have access to everything.

> "In the coming 30 years the tendency toward the dematerialized, the decentralized, the simultaneous, the platform enabled, and the cloud will continue unabated," he writes. "As long as the costs of communications and computation drop due to advances in technology, these trends are inevitable. They are the result of networks of communication expanding till they are global and ubiquitous, and as the networks deepen they gradually displace matter with intelligence."[1]

It won't matter where you live in the world, this access will be for everyone.

Other industry leaders predict the following:

- Access to the Internet will be universal. Connectivity will be constant and there will be no need for signing in to a particular stream.

- Cars will be seamlessly connected and allow users even more time to connect and communicate in traffic because they'll be self-driving.

- With everything online and apps running our lives, access to digital information will be needed for every facet of life, from payments, to work, to personal activities, and healthcare.

- Privacy will be available only if you are willing to pay extra for it.

- Information will find us instead of us needing to find it, in countless moments throughout our day.

Some of these predictions are already beginning to come true.

Attention Spans Will Remain Elusive

More and more information is competing for our attention.

Our brains feel divided, yet we somehow enjoy it. There's a reward when we see a comment on social media or a like or share online. Any type of immediate online response reaction (like liking, clicking, swiping, or sharing) increases the release of dopamine in the brain, which makes people more inclined to keep swiping, clicking, and scrolling.

Because most of these interfaces are impersonal and subject to our instantaneous and shifting reactions, our communication with each other becomes less personal, affecting how we view and interact with each other. It's harder to pay attention to people because they don't behave the way technology does. These interactions with devices and applications mimic personal connectivity but won't be real, giving us a false impression that we have a lot of friends or a lot of connections.

Our real, authentic, personal connections will decrease as we consume more noise.

With more interruptions from technology, it will be very hard for people to concentrate on the task at hand without being distracted.

Constant interruptions, continuous distractions, and persistent loss of focus will challenge leaders to engage and maintain focus on strategic objectives for long periods of time. If leaders can't accomplish this quickly, the likelihood of people losing interest and moving on to something else will increase. Parents and teachers will struggle too.

Our Minds Will Become Anemic and Impenetrable

It's really the game of chasing and consuming useless information. You're never getting to the core of something that has substantive value. You're consuming information that is superficial. You're never getting substance, just spending loads of time skimming the surface.

It's like drinking Diet Coke and eating popcorn all day long. If there isn't any substantial food in your diet, you will grow weak and get sick. That's what happens when people spend the majority of their time online or playing games and using social media. As technology becomes more pervasive and people spend more and more time consuming these barren brain calories, they will become empty mentally and emotionally.

They will become isolated, frustrated, and hungry.

Mentally anemic?

Consuming information mindlessly and incessantly is like eating popcorn and drinking diet soda. You feel filled but there's almost no mental nutrition.

When we give in to distractions, our brains are divided and start to weaken. When we can access information anywhere and anytime, our brain constantly looks for ways to snack rather than eat a healthy meal. We're nibbling on so much junk rather than focusing on a few things that are substantial and essential.

We quickly lose our focus and get in the habit of feeding on distractions rather than avoiding them.

Our brains then start to completely rewire themselves to seek the reward of ingesting empty information. It gets consistently tricked into thinking that it's filling itself with quality information, but it's just consuming useless information and dumbing itself down.

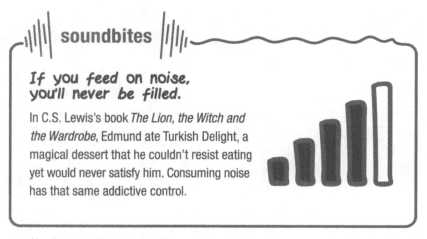

soundbites

If you feed on noise, you'll never be filled.

In C.S. Lewis's book *The Lion, the Witch and the Wardrobe*, Edmund ate Turkish Delight, a magical dessert that he couldn't resist eating yet would never satisfy him. Consuming noise has that same addictive control.

All of these factors and harmful effects rage around us—and within us. It's real and it hurts us all. Think about your diminishing focus in those terms. It is your brain, and you're really at risk.

[Brief Recap]

The nonstop noise of ubiquitous access to information is isolating us and shrinking our attention spans, overfilling our addicted minds with the empty calories of useless data.

{Tune-in}

There is an impending threat of losing focus as we constantly consume all this noise.

2 Huh? We're Going Collectively Deaf

We've all heard the expression "in one ear and out the other." It says everything about the tendency to tune out.

So where does this infamous phrase come from? Reportedly, the first recorded use was from Geoffrey Chaucer, the Father of English Literature, in his poem "Troilus and Criseyde" from the late fourteenth century.

The original is written in old English but is translated like this:

These words he said for the moment all/to help his friend, lest he for sorrow died:/doubtless to cause his woe to fall,/he cared not what nonsense he replied./But Troilus, who nigh for sorrow died,/ took little heed of anything he meant:/one ear heard it, at the other out it went.[1]

We can all relate to what Chaucer wrote. We've all tuned out information or chosen to ignore it, yet the reasons we do this varies from person to person.

So, Why Do We Tune Out? A Variety of Reasons

Here is a brief sampling of what's going on when we are so dialed in that we decide to check out:

- **"It really doesn't apply to me."**

  This reaction is driven primarily by relevance versus irrelevance. You don't need to pay attention when you are convinced the information is meant for someone else. If you have kids at home, this is the predictable response when you tell them that it's time to do the dinner dishes. "You clearly weren't talking to me, so I didn't even hear you ask."

- **"I was daydreaming and totally spaced out."**

  In a moment, your mind begins to wander, and everything you might hear instantly vanishes. Your brain goes elsewhere—to a magical place. This happens when people get stuck in a long meeting and "awaken" later to discover they didn't hear a single word. Or when they hear a safety announcement on a plane and drift off to think of other things.

- **"I don't agree at all with the person."**

  The tune-out is practically immediate when you don't share someone's opposing opinion or a distinct perspective. And the more they try to convince you that you are wrong, the faster your listening shuts down. Verbal sparring on talk radio provokes these responses, as do political debates.

- **"I don't understand at all. It is beyond my comprehension."**

  When a subject-matter expert starts to geek out and go into painfully deep details, you're forced to opt out of the conversation. Naturally, it feels like they're speaking a completely different language that is nearly incomprehensible. Trying to listen just reminds you how incapable you are of grasping the material. Imagine listening to a physics graduate student describing their doctoral dissertation when you barely passed high school science class.

- **"I choose to ignore because listening is too painful."**

After listening or reading a little, your brain hurts, and the pain is intolerable. This might be because the person is confusing, complaining, criticizing, or just all over the place. Realistically, there's pleasure in seeking silence and escaping from the "noise" they are generating.

- **"I already know everything."**

Talking to a know-it-all is no fun. There's no place for you to contribute when your thoughts are interrupted and finished midsentence. They know all the answers already. To continue along just means losing any small role you might have as the conversation gets hijacked, the tables are turned, and it turns into a monologue.

- **"I was preoccupied with something much more important."**

There are times when your head is dealing with urgent matters, like handling a crisis at home, working a complex problem, or planning an important career-defining event. In any of these moments, you might be incapable of hearing anything else that doesn't relate to what's squarely on your mind at the time. Imagine someone telling you about their weekend adventures when you're worried about having a tough conversation with your boss a few minutes later. You don't tune in because it goes in one ear and out the other.

What does this all mean? Our brains can't capture everything that's coming our way, for a variety of different reasons, in a host of distinct scenarios. You may have even more reasons than what's been shared here, but these are a few prominent ones.

The Impact of the "Elusive 600" on Our Listening

While we are having a conversation with someone or reading an e-mail, we can simultaneously be talking to ourselves in our head, maybe about the same subject or about something completely different. It's an inner monologue. It happens to all of us. Imagine what you're thinking when you feel what you're hearing is boring, complicated, or irrelevant.

At The BRIEF Lab, we teach a core concept called the "Elusive 600" that I learned from Sharon Ellis, a seasoned communications expert and close friend. Sharon blew my mind when she explained how the brain processes about 750 words per minute, yet the average person speaks or reads about 150 words per minute. In essence, our minds "overprocess" by 600 words per minute.

When I explain what happens in these terms, it makes sense to people. A lightbulb goes off, shining light on something they've all experienced yet had no term to explain. It's as if they are now aware of their awareness.

According to Ellis, while we are listening to someone talk, our brains start to say very specific things to us. In some moments, we tune in. "This is vital; I need to listen," or "How interesting," or "Is that a squirrel I just saw?" or "What am I going to have for lunch?" Yet, in many more cases, we just check out completely. "This doesn't apply to me," "I've heard this all before, and it was a waste of time," or "I don't follow what they're saying—I can't keep up." Whatever the triggered response, our Elusive 600 is a reality, and it needs to be managed.

► Our brains have the capacity to think faster than we speak.

Often the information we are processing isn't organized well, or at least our brain says it's not easy to follow. It shuts down and then shuts off. There might be too much information (TMI), or it is not in the right order, clearly presented in a way that requires minimal effort.

This is one of the reasons I wrote the book *BRIEF,* to help people present clear and concise information to a listener's Elusive 600, triggering the right responses, at the right moments, and minimizing the tendency of someone's brain to head in a completely different direction.

Imagine that you are on a video conference and the person speaking starts going off on a tangent. The "deep dive" information might be vital, but it triggers our Elusive 600 to say, "Hey, this sounds hard and confusing, I don't know where this is going. Maybe I should just take a coffee break."

It takes very little to trigger the Elusive 600 to work against, not for us.

How Words Become Worthless—and Triggers for a Tune-Out

This also happens when people use a lot of buzzwords when speaking. We hear these all of the time: "We need to move the goalpost" or "We have to empower our enterprise" or "We've gotta move the needle and run the numbers" or "We're sending cascading, relevant messaging to our key stakeholders" or "We need to find organic synergies."

When we speak this way, we trigger people to ignore us. To the Elusive 600, it sounds like static. Once this happens, it's almost impossible to regain their attention again.

Hard selling and persuasion don't work for me and probably don't for you. I have a saying—"tell me; don't sell me"—that I share in our courses. Nobody wakes up and wants to be sold, convinced, or swayed. It is an immediate turn off, and it sends the Elusive 600 into defense mode, looking for the catch and pushing back.

When you sense a person coming toward you, trying to win you over and overpower you, your mind is going to resist and your listening and demeanor change. The irony is that the more we try to be persuasive, the less our audience is going to hear. Statistics show that salespeople have a trustworthy rating of about 3%, and 9 out of 10 people dislike salespeople.[2] That doesn't mean you can't be convincing, but the harder you try, the less effective you are, because the audience's listening really starts to shrink.

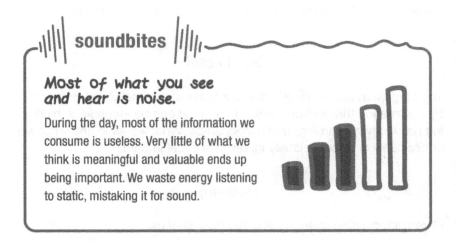

soundbites

Most of what you see and hear is noise.

During the day, most of the information we consume is useless. Very little of what we think is meaningful and valuable ends up being important. We waste energy listening to static, mistaking it for sound.

My Mom Thought I Had a Hearing Problem

An example from my own life paints the picture of what too much information and "noise" can do to a person.

I grew up in a large Catholic family. I'm the sixth of nine children. If you've ever been around big families, especially those with young children, you know there is a lot of clamor and chaos. When I was an infant, my mom worried that I might have a hearing problem because I wasn't reacting to verbal cues like my older siblings.

One day, a family friend was at the house. He was a doctor, so my mom shared her worries with him.

He asked her if she had a newspaper. The request momentarily puzzled my mom but she gave him one. He came to my crib, leaned over, and crumpled the newspaper by my ear. Immediately, I turned my head.

The doctor said to my mom, "Joe doesn't have a hearing problem. It's just loud around here. He's become immune to the noise."

Information overload is our noise. We are bombarded with it, and it affects us negatively and permanently. Some may feel they can live with it, almost like they're used to it, yet the noise is deafening and damaging, and we have to find ways to manage and mitigate it.

[Brief Recap]

The biggest threat we face is that our brain is so constantly bombarded by information that it shuts down. Tuning out can be immediate, hindering productivity, learning, and relationships. What we let in and what we consciously or unconsciously ignore has a real impact.

{Tune-in}

Listen, information overload is a threat to all of us.

3 Brain Basics: Are Your Penguins Falling Off the Iceberg?

My friend Chuck is a pararescueman (or PJ) in the US Air Force. He is as talented as he is humble. His responsibilities require him to master many different skills, ranging from combat operations to saving lives and aiding the injured, often in very austere and challenging environments. His profession requires constant training and, at any given moment, he might need to recall critical information like specific tactical procedures or complex medical techniques.

One day, he was telling me how he was trained to dig a snow cave to survive overnight in the cold. Another time he was telling me about different types of parachute equipment. Knowing how frequently he is in training, preparing for new missions and different scenarios, I asked him how he can focus on it all.

He said, "Joe, it's like penguins on an iceberg. You can only fit a certain number of them on there at a time. As I learn something new, a fat penguin falls off the other side. That's the way it goes."

Chuck's ability to focus, to learn—and relearn—critical information is essential for him to be prepared at all times, living up to the PJ
motto, "That others may live."

Our brains can't handle any more

Adding more
information into
your brain is like
getting penguins
on an iceberg.
As more are
added, others
are pushed off
the other side.

Our Brains Are Changing

Whether he knew it or not, he described what happens to our brains
with all of this noise and infobesity. It turns out that our brains aren't
just being affected but are changing, especially in the young, who are
exposed to infobesity from birth.

The human brain, which on average weighs about three pounds,
contains about 100 billion nerve cells that work like a big computer.[1]

The brain has three sections: the cerebrum, which controls things
like our conscious and unconscious thoughts and our speech and
hearing; the brain stem, which transmits information to the spinal
cord and controls eye movement and facial expressions; and the cer-
ebellum, which controls complex motor functions like walking.

The cerebrum is responsible for our ability to focus and remember things. We have three types of memory—long-term, short-term,
and working memory. It's our memory, particularly our short-term
and working memories, that are changing in this age of infobesity.

Short-term and working memory are closely linked. It's what we rely upon every day to focus on a presentation at work or on what our boss is telling us, to remember what time to pick up our kids from soccer or where we put our wallets. It's also what is disrupted by things like text messages, e-mail and social media alerts, and other common interruptions we face on a daily basis.

Working Memory in Decline

I want to focus on working memory because it's like the brain's version of random-access memory (RAM) in a computer. It is simply defined as the part of our short-term memory responsible for holding and managing information for mental processing, reasoning, and decision-making. Like RAM, it can decline when overtasked.

An easy way to understand it is to consider how many numbers you can temporarily store and recall. Years ago, people could easily retain many digits, but nowadays we struggle to remember phone numbers and addresses. When our focus is interrupted, research shows that that memory is wiped out. This function of the brain comes from the days when we had to react to immediate danger with a fight-or-flight response.

Imagine using a computer and opening numerous software applications, each demanding lots of processing power. The RAM won't be enough to handle all of it, and the speed will slow. The same is true for a mental task that requires focus. Interruptions are the equivalent of opening a new application as they create an attention deficit as the brain slows down to do two or more things at once.

In the workplace, interruptions are the norm. They can cause employees to take increased time to complete a task. A study by CBS News found that even a three-second interruption can cause twice as many errors—and twice the anxiety—for the workforce.[2] Author Kristin Wong from Lifehacker.com reports it takes about 25 minutes to get back into the swing of things after you've been interrupted.[3]

Got a minute?

► It takes 25 minutes to get back on task
   after an interruption.

Years ago, I worked closely on a marketing assignment for a Swedish software company, Cogmed, that conducted extensive research to prove one could train the brain and regain lost working memory capacity. Its program and studies were encouraging because they helped people regain lost capacity to focus, a critical skill to be successful.

In an attempt to get more done in an environment of constant e-mails, text messages, social media, and 24-hour news, we attempt to excel at multitasking, thinking we can juggle many things at once. Our smartphones are always with us so the interruptions are right there as we switch rapidly from one task to another with little focus and declining efficiency.

A strong or weak working memory can spell the difference.

Brains Are Like Computers

If we look at the brain like a computer, we realize that when we try to process more information than our working memory can handle, our minds slow down. We become forgetful, inefficient, and we feel as if a fog is clouding our minds.

My kids laugh at me because when they look at my smartphone, they remark, "Dad, look at how many apps you have open." My reply is always the same—I forget to close them. I fail to recognize that my phone slows down, sometimes to a stop. It's no surprise that when I close them, my phone works better and faster. It's the same with our brain.

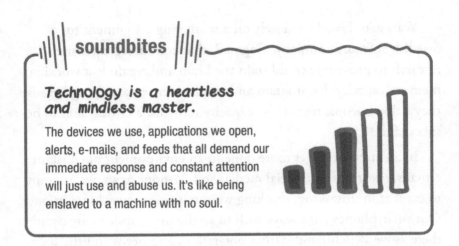

Another way to show what is happening to our working memory is to consider our ability to hold a string of numbers, such as phone numbers, in our heads. Typically, phone numbers are 10 or 11 digits long.

Research shows that our working memory can retain only 7 items at a time.[4] As my Air Force friend would put it, penguins are being bumped off the iceberg all day long.

When was the last time you tried to recall a phone number instead of using speed dial or your phone's contacts or call records? What happens when you meet someone and they tell you their name, but you instantly forget it?

Our minds seem to be weakening as we rely more and more on technology to manage these tasks.

Back in the day, we used to handle all those details minute to minute with sharper attention. Though that ability naturally declines as people get older, researchers have found that, because our brains are so saturated with information coming at us, our ability to retain a string of digits in the moment, like phone numbers, social security numbers, or a friend's address, is shrinking.

Our focus is in decline.

We're Losing Impulse Control

Not only is our attention altering, but so is our ability to control our impulses.

Studies cited by Daniel J. Levitin, author of *The Organized Mind: Thinking Straight in the Age of Information Overload,* show that multitasking creates a dopamine-addiction feedback loop that rewards us for our inattention.[5] In essence, you're getting rewarded for losing focus because you're looking for new stimulation, new dopamine releases.

A way to understand this better is to consider what happens to babies when we try to distract them from crying by waving a bright or shiny object in front of them.

Glenn Wilson, a former visiting professor of psychology at Gresham College in London, England, found that multitasking reduces IQ by 10 points. In an article entitled "Info-mania Dents IQ More Than Marijuana," he asserts that the cognitive loss in multitasking is greater than what is lost when a person smokes marijuana.[6]

Earl Miller, a neuroscientist at MIT and a leading authority in divided attention, in an NPR article entitled "Think You're Multitasking? Think Again!," says, "People can't do [multitasking] very well, and when they say they can, they're deluding themselves."[7]

Levitin echoes their observations, stating, "make no mistake: e-mail, Facebook- and Twitter-checking constitute a neural addiction."[8]

Over time, all these interruptions make it harder for us to focus our attention or think about something for a sustained amount of time.

Our Brains Get Hooked

What makes it hard to change these habits and to improve our focus is that our brains have become, in many ways, addicted to these interruptions. In some instances, as was the case in the creation of many popular social media apps and video games, companies have designed applications and technology to get us hooked.

They are tapping into a chemical in our brains called dopamine. *Psychology Today* defines it as "a neurotransmitter that helps control the brain's reward and pleasure centers. Dopamine also helps regulate movement and emotional responses, and it enables us not only to see rewards, but also to take action to move toward them."[9]

Dopamine is at the root of all feelings of pleasure and is what increases when a person is addicted to something. Our smartphones feed into what behavioral scientist Susan Weinschenk calls a "dopamine loop."

"When you bring up the feed on one of your favorite apps, the dopamine loop has become engaged. With every photo you scroll through, headline you read, or link you go to, you are feeding the loop, which just makes you want more. It takes a lot to reach satiation, and in fact you might never be satisfied," she says.[10]

According to the American Psychiatric Association, addiction is defined as an excessive use of a substance—in this case, we're talking about the Internet, social media, news feeds, texting—that leads to impairment of everyday life, sleep, and relationships. Statistically, it's pretty staggering. Up to 18% of people, according to some research are actually addicted to the Internet.[11]

Sean Parker, who was one of the early founders of Facebook, infamously said, "God only knows what this is doing to our brains." Many popular apps and games are exploiting the psychological vulnerabilities within us by offering instant gratification through this feedback loop—this addictive feedback loop of dopamine—to get these releases."[12]

··{ NOTEWORTHY }·····························

Addicted by design
Adam Alter decodes the business of getting us hooked

Traditional addictions like smoking, drinking, and drugs now have new, nasty companions. Smartphones, wearable devices, video games, social media, and online shopping are also competing—and winning over—our attention in novel, destructive ways.

In his book *Irresistible*, Adam Alter tackles the rise of addictive technology.

As a professor of marketing and psychology, Alter not only delves into these new addictions but also reveals the business behind them.

"Tech isn't morally good or bad until it is wielded by the corporations that fashion it for mass consumption," he says. "Apps and platforms can be designed to promote rich social connections; or, like cigarettes, they can be designed to addict."

He deciphers hidden designs that contain six basic ingredients that drive any behavioral addiction: compelling goals; irresistible, positive feedback; incremental progress; rising difficulty over time; demand for resolution; and strong social connections.

While technology is clearly making our lives more convenient, he adds that it is also excessively alluring.

"Life is more convenient than ever, but convenience has also weaponized temptation," he cautions. "Each month almost one hundred hours (are) lost to checking e-mail, texting, playing games, surfing the web, reading articles, checking bank balances, and so on. Over the average lifetime, that amounts to a staggering 11 years."

He captures in great detail the rise of behavioral addictions and the biology and business behind it, while making a compelling case that we are all susceptible to becoming addicts. His tone is serious and the evidence strong; these bonds are hard to break once they're fashioned in our day-to-day lives.

Bottom line: Alter's book is noteworthy because it shines a light on how technology—in its many shapes and sizes—is engineered to hook us.

How Often Do We Check Our Smartphones?

Smartphone usage is staggering. Seventy percent of young smartphone users check their phone three or more times an hour. Twenty-two percent of them are checking it every few minutes.[13] According to *Dscout's* "Putting a Finger on Our Phone Obsession," on average, people tap, swipe, and click their phones 2,617 times per day; the heaviest users do so 5,427 times per day.[14] If you are looking at certain groups of people, certainly college–aged and high school–aged people, the phone in the hand is a constant. They've learned to live with it because that's all they've known. But even people who have not used smartphones all their lives have difficulty resisting the urge to frequently check them throughout the day. A *TechTalk* survey recorded that 6% checked their work e-mail while their spouse was in labor and another 6% had checked e-mail at a funeral![15]

Hand it over!

The average user manages to swipe/click/tap a smartphone 2,617 times a day. Heaviest users do that 5,427 times.

We did a research study at The BRIEF Lab and found that 70% of people check their phones as soon as they wake up in the morning and right before they go to bed.[16]

Here are five questions to ask yourself if you think you might be addicted to your phone:

1. Am I glued to my phone?
2. Can I put my phone down—even for a bit?
3. Do I feel withdrawal symptoms if I'm not using it?
4. Am I sneaking use of my phone?
5. Do I use my phone when bored or depressed?

Why is all of this important?

Our ability to focus and concentrate is critical to the things that we need to do well every day. Say, for example, you're in a meeting and somebody's talking to you but your mind doesn't focus on what they are saying because you are thinking of several other things. Or you are on the phone talking to a family member and you start watching a bird eat a worm, rather than listening to the caller. Or you have to concentrate to prepare an important presentation and you keep getting up to do other things. You aren't paying attention to those things completely so you do them poorly, they take longer to do, and doing them tires you out.

This divided attention can have disastrous results both professionally and personally.

[Brief Recap]

Consuming information at an increasingly alarming rate is changing and reshaping our brains. How we are clinging to technology is affecting how we focus, how we concentrate and, fundamentally, how we think.

{Tune-in}

As our brains are changing, we must make crucial decisions on how we protect them from the addictive allure of technology.

4 Living in an Info Junkie Crack House

I f we think there's too much information or too many devices or distractions causing us to lose our focus, just imagine when virtual reality (VR) becomes a pervasive part of everyday life.

VR is already here and pounding on the door to come in.

Let's take a closer look at what awaits us. VR is a computer-generated simulation of a three-dimensional image or environment that can be interacted with in a seemingly real or physical way by a person using special electronic equipment, such as a helmet with a screen inside or gloves fitted with sensors.[1]

Forget about looking at screens; you're wearing it and you're immersed.

Multibillion-dollar companies like Facebook, Google, and Microsoft already have affordable virtual reality technologies and more are on the way. Consumers have purchased millions of the headsets, which cover your eyes, blind you to the world around you, and trick your brain into thinking what it is seeing is a new, "real" world.

Now, I'm not saying that this technology is all bad—far from it. VR can be used in video gaming and also in education and training for a wide variety of applications like sports, medicine, and combat. Its promise and primary selling point is that it's much more realistic than anything we've experienced previously.

However, if we're concerned about how our brains are reacting to technology and how addictive its use can be, through VR, things will only get worse unless we moderate its use.

It's a promise, and it's also a curse.

Training and Education Will Be the Gateway Drug

One of the foremost experts on virtual reality is Stanford University professor Jeremy Bailenson, who wrote *Experience on Demand: What Virtual Reality Is, How It Works, and What It Can Do*. Bailenson is the founding director of the Virtual Human Interactive Lab at Stanford.

In his book, he notes the positive and negative dimensions of virtual reality.

He writes that one of the primary applications of VR will be in education. You're going to learn by doing. They call this embodied cognition. This can be a good thing because it is much more impactful than traditional learning.

One use may be when science teachers are presenting a unit on Mars. Instead of watching a video or reading about the planet, students will don virtual reality technology and be transported there. You don't talk about the planet; you go there.

Athletes are already using virtual reality headsets to simulate training. The athlete is in a moment that is virtual, yet the brain thinks it's real and he or she can go through the steps or the motions of an activity—throwing a baseball to home plate, playing in a high-stakes football game, or whatever the task might be—and create or recreate what that would feel like in that circumstance or pressure-filled moment. The possibilities to create scenarios seem limitless.

It's starting to get unreal

Virtual reality will be the promise of next-generation educators and may be the dumbing down of society.

Impending Health Impacts?

However, doctors and researchers are already concerned about the health implications of virtual reality, such as its effects on the eye, the nervous system, and on children. Many VR devices include a warning to see a doctor before using them if you are pregnant, elderly, or have a pre-existing condition like a heart condition, vision abnormalities, or psychiatric disorders.

We must examine the negative aspects before we fully embrace the positives of this technology.

"There are a variety of potential issues. One is how we affect the growth of the eye, which can lead to myopia or nearsightedness,"[2] observes Martin Banks, who studies the impact virtual environments have on vision, at the University of California, Berkeley.

There already is evidence that doing close-up work, such as looking at tablets and phones, increases the risk for nearsightedness. It is also changing how the brain interprets how we are communicating.

"In a virtual environment, the way we look and interact is changed because we may be projecting onto the eyes something that looks far away, but in reality, it's only a few centimeters from the eye," says Walter Greenleaf, a behavioral neuroscientist who has studied VR in medical settings for over 30 years.[3]

Science calls that the vergence-accommodation conflict and isn't quite sure how serious it might be. "We're tricking the brain," said Greenleaf, who works with Stanford University's Virtual Human Interaction Lab, "and we don't know the long-term effect of this."[4]

Ironically, in an interview, Jeremy Bailenson revealed that while he uses virtual reality himself and on subjects in his lab, he has allowed his six-year-old daughter to use it only four times and only for five minutes at a time.

A Potential Threat to Consider

Why might virtual reality be a curse? We are already seeing the negative impact of information addiction. There's noise everywhere, and our brains crave distractions and multitasking. With VR, we live in a kind of info crack house. Virtual reality makes the user feel like they are escaping from their world, which is often harsh, and entering a virtual world, which is seemingly better.

That is troubling; it has a deep addictive allure.

Imagine kids who don the headset and start doing homework but get distracted and start doing something else. Their parents are helpless—standing on the outside—because they think their kids are learning. Who wants to be against a new way of learning?

Virtual reality has the potential to isolate people from each other even more. For example, in February 2016, Facebook founder Mark Zuckerberg walked down the aisle at a conference for Samsung in Barcelona, Spain. The thousands of attendees were wearing virtual reality headsets, and no one noticed him.

A photo of this went viral. When asked by a German reporter to answer critics who felt it showed that the virtual reality experience is isolating and not a socially collective experience that people say it is, Zuckerberg replied:

I think people tend to be worried about every new technology that comes along. Critics worry that if we spend time paying attention to that new kind of media or technology instead of talking to each other that it is somehow isolating, but humans are fundamentally social. So, I think in reality if a technology doesn't actually help us socially understand each other better it isn't going to catch on and succeed. You could probably go all the way back to the first books. I bet people said, "Why should you read when you could talk to other people?" The point of reading is that you get to deeply immerse yourself in a person's perspective, right? Same thing with newspapers, phones or TVs. Soon it will be virtual reality I bet.[5]

Zuckerberg's reply is flawed, and his motivations may be questionable.

Books aren't addictive; they're interesting. TVs, phones (via a landline), and newspapers are mildly addictive. Newspapers are hardly as addictive as TVs, nor is a phone as addictive as a smart-phone. The continuum of going from books to newspapers to TVs to smartphones and now to virtual reality is a continuum of addiction. Virtual reality goes far down that line to a place where hardware and software developers may have found the ultimate hook: leave your world and get addicted to theirs.

While people are hooked to smartphones, the Internet, and social media, VR represents this promise and curse of living in an immersive world of never-ending noise consumption.

It's an info junkie crack house.

Who Can Stop This?

Education will be the entry point for making VR part of our daily lives. In the same way that kids go to school now, with tablets and laptops and learning on screens, they will put on headsets and learn in virtual reality. While in school, they will start to live, little by little, more in this new reality and less in their own lives.

Parents will feel helpless to stop it.

In the heart of Silicon Valley is the Waldorf School of the Peninsula, a pre-K through high school private institution that does not use tech devices like smartphones or tablets. The choices that parents working in tech giants like Google, Apple, and Yahoo make for their own children should alert us to these dangers.

Some researches even question if technology really makes children better learners.

A study by the international Organisation for Economic Co-operation and Development found "that even countries which have invested heavily in information and communication technologies for education have seen no noticeable improvement in their performances."[6]

Some groups are stepping forward in an effort to protect children from this continuum of addiction. In 2018, major investors of Apple called on the company to help curb children's addictions to smartphones. The company said it would implement more "parental controls."

Will this be enough?

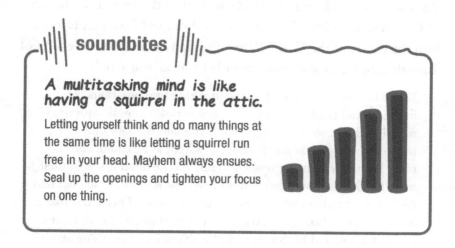

‖‖‖ **soundbites** ‖‖‖

A multitasking mind is like having a squirrel in the attic.

Letting yourself think and do many things at the same time is like letting a squirrel run free in your head. Mayhem always ensues. Seal up the openings and tighten your focus on one thing.

More Brain Celery

We need to recognize that VR does not impact our minds and emotions in the same way as applications, screens, and technology today are designed to addict us. Although it has an inherently addictive power, virtual reality goes further and isolates even more.

You seal yourself off.

Of course, we want our children to learn through new experiences, but can they resist the temptation of spending more time in the virtual world than their own? Surely, technology companies will want to hook them hard so they play, explore, and learn there all day.

And what will they be seeing and consuming through VR? Mostly noise—brain celery. Celery is said to have nearly zero calories because of the energy is takes to eat it. As mentioned in a previous chapter, we feed our brains empty calories and become mentally and emotionally anemic.

When I think of what immersive access to information and entertainment does to our brains I recall a scene from C.S. Lewis's book *The Lion, the Witch and the Wardrobe,* part of the famous Chronicles of Narnia series. One of the characters, Edmund Pevensie, is lured into the power of the White Witch through an enchanted version of Turkish delight, a sweet made mainly of sugar and starch:

> While he was eating the Queen kept asking him questions. At first Edmund tried to remember that it is rude to speak with one's mouth full, but soon he forgot about this and thought only of trying to shovel down as much Turkish Delight as he could, and the more he ate the more he wanted to eat, and he never asked himself why the Queen should be so inquisitive. She got him to tell her that he had one brother and two sisters, and that one of his sisters had already been in Narnia and had met a Faun there, and that no one except himself and his brother and his sisters knew anything about Narnia. She seemed especially interested in the fact that there were four of them and kept on coming back to it.[7]

Edmund is so consumed with eating more Turkish delight that he starts to give up his willpower with each bite. That's what virtual reality might be like for us.

It's a potential nightmare.

We have to see the threat. Yes, there might be information that I need, but there's a lot of it that I don't. There's a lot of noise consumption. Yes, there's learning, but there's also addiction. We're conceding our willpower to the promise of education and entertainment, only to fall into the trap of seriously addictive behavior.

More information anxiety is coming our way. Virtual reality is not a fad.

[Brief Recap]

Virtual reality can be amazing but also amazingly addictive. Since VR essentially tricks the brain, we need to be aware of the damaging physical and mental effects of such an immersive, isolating, and addictive platform.

{Tune-in}

We must guard against being enticed by the initial appeal of virtual reality. Protect your brain. Protect your perspective.

Part Two

The Big Tune-Out Is Coming (Imagining the Unthinkable—Six Short Stories to Wake You Up)

5 Always Stuck at School

W hile I shared with people the motivation behind this book, several have divulged some startling stories with me. Such is the case with my friend Bryan, who thought he lost his teenage daughter to depression.

Bryan and his wife Anna seemed to have model children. Their son and daughter are overachievers by anyone's standards. They do well in school, have tons of friends, and are well adjusted.

Or so Bryan and Anna thought, until their daughter Monica, the younger of the two children, was a junior in high school and started missing school. She refused to go and even stopped wanting to get out of bed.

Anxiety and depression had engulfed her. It was bad. She missed so much school that she was on the edge of failing out. There was no sign she was ever going to go back. Her parents felt helpless, looking for reasons.

Monica would isolate herself in her room each day not doing anything. She wouldn't read, wouldn't check social media, wouldn't watch TV.

As soon as this started, Bryan and Anna got her into therapy and tried everything they could to help their daughter. Nothing was working. They thought they were losing her.

Serious Triggers

In desperation, they sent her to a private girls' school in the Northwest that focused on helping girls with addictions, behavioral problems, and other trauma. At the school, the students were completely unplugged from social media and technology. There were consequences for failing to follow the rules, and it was a very structured environment.

Monica's time at the new school saved her life. She surfaced from the depression and now has more energy and focus because she has rules and strategies to control her behavior. Going back to her previous school was only possible because she was able to break the cycle.

It seems that social media was a powerful, primary trigger for her depression.

At any moment of any day she felt pressured to be "always on"—sharing updates, photos, liking posts, and counting how many days she was on. She couldn't escape it. It was like she was in school all day long. Her identity was wrapped up in connecting with her peers all day. The irony is her constant connectedness created isolation. Monica spiraled down into a terrible anxiety and depression cycle where she felt completely paralyzed.

New Protective Behaviors

The last time I spoke to my friend, his daughter was coming home from the school. But before she could come back and resume her life, she had to make a personal plan to handle everyday teenage situations, like what she would do when her friends would go out to eat and they'd all be on their smartphones using social media.

How would she resist this behavior? How was she going to cope when her peers are almost always plugged in? How would she say no and set boundaries?

Before this all happened, Monica was always on social media, connecting with people, commenting on their posts, and posting herself. The pressure to make everyone "like" her posts and to present an exciting portrayal of her life was overwhelming. It turns out this created a massive wave of depression and anxiety for her.

She was absolutely miserable. Once they learned what was wrong with Monica, Bryan and Anna realized they enabled her behavior, thinking all that time spent glued to her phone wasn't harmful but part of being a modern teen.

Terrified Parents

What's frightening for parents is that what happened to Monica is happening to other children with alarming regularity. And with the predictions that access to technology will only increase in the future, parents will have to be vigilant to protect their kids.

In past generations, when students left school, they also left behind anxieties or stress related to their classes. There was a separation. Not anymore.

One of my sons tells me, "Dad, we're always at school because we're connected to the technology even when we're at home." He's right and it's a reality.

All those comments, likes, shares, and posts make our children feel like they constantly have to keep up to be "on" and be accepted. They feel stuck at school with:

- Online homework postings and assignments
- Discussion boards where students *must* be online and interact to complete assignments
- Teacher e-mails and homework posts
- Online books and articles
- Reliance on laptops, even in the elementary school
- Persistent, online bullying (you can't escape the playground bully—even at home)
- Negative online posts and taunts from other schools/students regarding athletic teams and other activities

Disturbing Statistics

What makes kids so vulnerable to technology addiction is that their brains are still developing. We know that teens have underdeveloped impulse control and empathy judgment. Their brains are incredibly malleable and able to change to their environments.

They also have what neurologists call "a hyperactive risk-reward system" that makes them susceptible to addiction.

Mindfilled at home

► It's easy to let our minds wander aimlessly from one thing to the next.

The part of our brains that helps us to focus and understand human emotion doesn't completely develop until well into our twenties, says Paul Atchley, a professor of psychology at the University of Kansas.

"During our teenage years, it's important to train that prefrontal cortex not to be easily distracted," Atchley said in a *Time* magazine interview. "What we're seeing in our work is that young people are constantly distracted, and also less sensitive to the emotions of others." This training, though, may seem like a daunting task when kids are hindered by these technological distractions.[1]

Our Children in Isolation

Any person just looking around can see how technology is making our kids more isolated. You see groups of kids in a restaurant or in a park, and they aren't talking to each other, at least not verbally interacting or making eye contact. Their heads are down, and their fingers are quickly moving over their screens.

Most of what people post on social media are positive things, yet they contribute to young people's anxiety and depression. No one wants to look bad or ridiculed. They're not sharing the difficulties of adolescence but are trying to keep up and look good. This fuels the desire, especially among adolescent girls, for acceptance, for the need to be "perfect" and FOMO (the fear of missing out). You have to stay on and keep up or you get left behind.

That's hurting our children.

Between 2010 and 2016, the number of adolescents who experienced at least one major depressive episode leapt by 60%, according to the US Department of Health and Human Services (DHHS). Depression is certainly on the rise. In a 2016 survey of 17,000 kids, the DHHS also found that about 13% of adolescents had a major depressive episode, compared to the 8% reported in 2010.[2]

The rate of suicide is also increasing among people age 10 to 19, according to the Centers for Disease Control and Prevention. Young women are suffering most.[3]

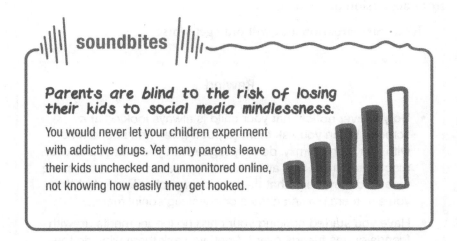

soundbites

Parents are blind to the risk of losing their kids to social media mindlessness.

You would never let your children experiment with addictive drugs. Yet many parents leave their kids unchecked and unmonitored online, not knowing how easily they get hooked.

A study by San Diego State University "found that kids who spent three hours or more a day on smartphones or other electronic devices were 34% more likely to suffer at least one suicide-related outcome—including feeling hopeless or seriously considering suicide—than kids who used devices two hours a day or less. Among kids who used electronic devices five or more hours a day, 48% had at least one suicide-related outcome."[4]

Is It Addiction?

Although medical professionals debate whether teens overusing social media or video games can be labeled an addiction, they agree that overuse can have adverse effects on young people.

Dr. Michael Bishop, who runs Summerland camps for young people ages 10 to 18 who have video game or technology addictions, told National Public Radio that teens who come to him fall into two broad categories: (1) those who spend so much time playing video games that they lose their social skills, and (2) those who overuse social media, who are most often girls.[5]

The kids into gaming are most often boys, and they often suffer from depression or anxiety.

It's a scary situation and will only get worse.

Rewind

- Do you ever notice that your child is always looking at a screen? When you ask them to put it away and spend time with you or the family, do they argue with you that you're over-reacting or argue that all of their friends are online at the same time? Do they claim that they are doing schoolwork, but then you see them playing games or checking social media?

- Have you started noticing your child no longer meets up with friends or has friends over? When you ask them why, do they become aggressive, saying they are meeting with their friends online?

- Have you noticed that after you've confiscated your child's phone or device in order to get them away from the screen, they become edgy, aggressive, or withdrawn? Have you found them secretly using your phone or their siblings' device?

- Have you considered the effects of your own phone habits on your children's behavior?

[Brief Recap]

There's an alarming rise in anxiety and depression for teens, much triggered by the always-on, addictive nature of smartphones and social media. Our youth feel constantly connected to digital devices, yet more isolated from each other at a time in their lives where they need to develop personally, socially, and emotionally in healthy ways.

{Tune-in}

We need to have a heightened awareness of the behavioral impact that constant connectivity has on our kids and find practical ways to protect (and disconnect) them.

6 A Misleading Leader

Jonas didn't think he would fail so miserably. The career-defining moment when he would orchestrate an acquisition touted as a "merger of equals" seemed like a done deal.

"He read the crowd and all the key players wrong," his former head of strategy, Paula, said, looking back on the year since the purchase. "Jonas felt so strongly that his communication and change management teams would get everyone onboard and working to integrate the two companies. He missed dozens of early warning signs."

The deal had been years in the making, with a few key players making all the bold, behind-the-scenes moves. When all the financials were agreed to, they quickly raced to formulate a press release that would set the terms and create some buzz in the market. Like many deals like this, there was a lot of wishful thinking that people on both sides would embrace the "synergies" and follow their leadership teams forward.

"When the announcement was made, it was all hype, energy, and spin," Paula lamented. "None of the people who had a stake in the event knew why the deal was made, and many worried that it wasn't a blending of two companies at all but an acquisition that would crush one culture and never get teams working together."

The damage from the overflow of information, and the subsequent noise created, undermined any chance of understanding and success.

Streaming Information

In the weeks and months after the announcement, the communication poured out systematically, as Jonas had planned. There was a steady stream of e-mail blasts, town-hall meetings, social media posts, video tutorials, and cascading messages that flowed from the "war room" with strategic purpose and precision. Change management teams performed flawlessly, following an elaborate process and meeting all key milestones, deadlines, and deliverables.

"Jonas wanted to be transparent and overcommunicate to everyone. And that's what happened," Paula said. "People started getting buried with information and started to feel it."

Meeting mayhem

Professionals spend an average of 23 hours a week in meetings.

BLAH. BLAH. BLAH BLAH. BLAH. BLAH

Losing Momentum

Many workers felt excited at first but started losing enthusiasm as the communication from above felt one-sided and too much like a sales pitch.

"I just didn't know what information was the most important and what I was supposed to act on," said Tobias, a veteran marketing specialist at the company. "We had all these meetings and updates, but there was no clear guidance on priorities. We all talked about it around the office. When a new action plan was sent out, we'd look out our cubicles at each other and say, almost unanimously, 'Did you understand that?' We'd all respond, 'Nope!'"

This wasn't the first major launch Tobias worked on. He's had years of experience, but even he couldn't decipher the message.

In meetings, employees weren't asked to provide input as much as spend time consuming updates and convincing their subordinates and cross-functional teams with even more communication. The process flowed from the top down, pushing out updates, but not moderating feedback nor adjusting the approach.

"The directives kept on coming. I wanted to say something, but the message communicated to us in meetings was that everything was handled already. This started to make me worry because that's not how it worked with the successful launches I had worked on. There were always opportunities for feedback, adjustments, and questions in the past," Tobias said.

E-mail is a great source of noise

51% of people delete e-mail within two seconds of opening it.

Powerful Monologue

"They buried any spark of enthusiasm and acceptance with a fire hose of internal communication," Paula said. "It was a powerful monologue that just fell on deaf ears. And that's when things went from bad to worse."

Morale started to become an issue as people were spending so much time in meetings that they couldn't work. The expected layoffs didn't help either as the rumor mill spun into high gear.

"There was nothing wrong with the initial idea. It seemed justified. But when they brought me in halfway through the process, I noticed the telltale signs of failure," said Sandra, a consultant hired to help with the rollout. "The employees were drowning in too much information. Although they believed in the company's efforts, they had become fatigued by all of the data dumps, e-mails, the endless meetings, and working late nights and weekends without feeling like they were accomplishing anything."

··{ NOTEWORTHY } ·····························

High-performance noise reducers
Arriving ready to be at your best

Scott Peltin, author of *Sink, Float or Swim*, wants to make sure that professionals always show up at their best.

He's an expert in helping pros around the world achieve high-performance results and firmly contends that if you're cognitively fatigued ("brain fogged," as he calls it) from overwhelming decision-making, constantly having long periods of concentration—without any time for recovery—it will be impossible for you to turn down the noise.

Beyond that, he warns against emotional fatigue.

"It makes us all the worst. And that can come from everything from jet lag and sleep deprivation to allowing things to take you on an emotional roller coaster ride that you're not supposed to be on, so you get hijacked emotionally," Scott warns. "And then when you do that, your brain is hyperactive, looking for noise, because it's in survival mode. And in survival mode, any noise can be a threat to your life."

He works with leaders to help them learn ways to constantly recalibrate themselves, making sure that they're fully recovered, and always at their best.

"It requires a purposeful vision of me at my best," he says. "If not, I'm at the whim of everything else around me."

Bottom line: This thought leader is noteworthy because he makes a strong correlation between emotional, physical, and cognitive fatigue and how those conditions make us more susceptible to noise.

All Talk, No Action

Fear, confusion, and mistrust ensued as employees listened to executive leadership navigate the change. Jonas felt strongly that putting more information out to people would be helpful, never realizing how he started a process that submerged them, greatly diminishing any chance of long-term success. It just became more noise and very little sound of clear direction. Talk didn't lead to action but to more talk, discussion, and murmuring.

"It was like the more management talked, the more people would tune them out," Sandra concluded, looking back on the year-long integration process. "People were tapped out and started tuning out. Their interest and their attention tanks were empty."

It wasn't that employees didn't try to understand. They were just overfed with too much information.

Rewind

- As a leader, when you think your employees are excited about what you're saying in a meeting or presentation and nodding their heads, are you sure they are all on board?

- Do you give your employees an opportunity to have a dialogue about what you are presenting, or is it strictly one way, with you doing most of the talking?

- Do you moderate the amount of information being passed on to your employees so that they don't get overwhelmed and so that the message isn't lost in over explanation?

- Do you have steps in place to provide participants an opportunity to give feedback?

[Brief Recap]

In attempts to be transparent, an overload of information, most of it excessive and irrelevant, can impede understanding, frustrate people, and cause them to tune out due to frustration and lack of ownership in the process.

{Tune-in}

Tell me; don't sell me! Get my feedback along the way. Tell me the *what*, the *why,* and the *so what*.

7 The Loss of Civil Discourse

Watching television wasn't how Rebecca usually spent her evenings. She was typically busy after work with friends, volunteering, and going to grad school. It was a rainy Monday night, and Rebecca was exhausted after a long day at work. She had lots of meetings and project work and was glued to her phone, e-mailing teammates all day, and checking on a new vendor.

Rebecca didn't want to see her smartphone anymore, not even to check social media or to text a friend, something she'd instinctively do to relax and kill time. She was communicating so much during the day that she felt like her phone was an extension of work, so she ditched it and turned on cable news, something totally different.

Her Civic Duty

What she saw on one of the first news stations caught her eye. It was a political debate. Since it was election season, she thought it was her responsibility as a taxpayer to tune in and hear the issues.

"I went in with an open mind," she confessed. "I have opinions, of course, but I really wanted to hear the facts explained from different points of view."

Paul, the first candidate, opened with a vicious, personal attack on Stacey, his opponent. Stacey responded by cutting Paul off, mid-sentence. The facilitator looked flustered and tried to intervene and create a balanced conversation.

It didn't work.

Stacey knew Paul's negative comments might cast a cloud on her character and sway undecided voters, maybe bringing people like Rebecca to his side. So, Stacey fought back, quickly and viciously, to show her strength against the incumbent's critical comments.

"He started attacking her and I didn't even hear what his original point was, just that his tone was so aggressive," Rebecca recalled. "Instantly, I felt she was being mistreated but she responded just like him. She harshly counterattacked. It all started to get pretty ugly but I wanted to hear their points so I decided to sit tight and watch more of the debate."

Uninformed and Confused

As the exchanges continued, Rebecca struggled to follow their points or to be even mildly persuaded. She felt tugged like she was stuck between two quarreling parents and was left uninformed and deeply confused. Her mind wandered, and she started looking at the candidates' wardrobes and stopped listening to what they were saying. The facilitator was funny, she thought, as the heated exchanges didn't cease and became almost comical.

Over the course of the next 10 minutes, Rebecca witnessed facts mixed with feelings, commentary that became personal criticism, and respect and listening give way to impulse and interruptions.

"I tried so hard to listen to them and learn the issues, but my brain hurt," she admitted. "As part of the TV audience, I felt like I was in the middle of the abuse. It made me sick, and it was impossible to hear their comments because they talked over each other."

No Respect

Civility was thrown out the window. Respect was seen as a sign of weakness. Emotion superseded logic. Screaming seemed permissible. People talked at and over each other, and neither person was inclined to listen to what the other one was saying.

Acknowledging a comment was admitting defeat.

The entire experience left Rebecca back on the outside, wondering if this was a rare, wild exchange. The next day at work, she commented to several co-workers about the debate and how crazy it got. Unfortunately for Rebecca, her two colleagues were on the opposite ends of the political spectrum. They missed the underlying lack of civility and only saw their candidate as the victor, not the villain.

"I thought I'd make small talk the next morning about a rude political exchange, and I opened a can of worms," Rebecca said. "They started trying to convince each other that their candidate won and had a futile debate that sounded like the one on TV. Nobody was listening."

Tower of Babel

Exchanges like this happen every day. People hear an opposing view, and their response is not to listen but to disagree. It's as if we live in a Tower of Babel where everyone is speaking a different language and people can't hear or find common ground.

It all becomes noise.

Morals, views, and opinions should be held and strongly defended, of course. Yet the loss of civil discourse is troubling. People tune each other out instantaneously. One word is a trigger to shut someone off.

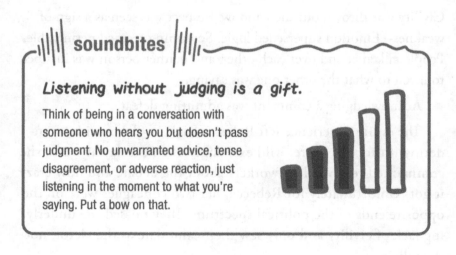

soundbites

Listening without judging is a gift.

Think of being in a conversation with someone who hears you but doesn't pass judgment. No unwarranted advice, tense disagreement, or adverse reaction, just listening in the moment to what you're saying. Put a bow on that.

Catching Her Attention

Ironically, on her drive home that night, Rebecca heard a remarkable political ad on the radio. It caught her attention in so many ways. This is what she heard:

> Well, here we go again. Another election. This one is for keeps. This time your vote will decide who will be our next sheriff. Hello, I'm John Z. I'm backing Steve Adams for sheriff of Moore County. We have three good men running in the general election. One thing makes Steve stand out: Steve has new ideas. He brings something to the office that we need more of: a businessperson's way of looking at things. As you begin to hear these announcements between now and election day, please don't block them out. Obviously, we need good strong honest law enforcement from our sheriff. We also need, and it's the same thing we need throughout government, ways to save money.
>
> Steve Adams has some good solid plans to do just that. Now there will be talk that Steve is not a cop, and he's not. Most people who administer hospitals are not doctors, and the heads of the FBI are not FBI agents, and this goes on. Steve will have the best people he can find to run that end of the office. That will leave him free to take care of you by listening to you, and by being a good steward with your tax money while saving you millions, yes millions, of dollars. So, I hope you keep an open mind; that's all I ask of any voter. Listen, and in fact, give him a call—talk to him. I think you'll like what you hear, and you might even end up like me—supporting Steve Adams for sheriff.[1]

Why did she listen to John Z.? First, he admitted they all were good candidates. Second, he acknowledged people might tune out or ignore Steve's candidacy because he was an outsider. Third, he wasn't being pushy or aggressive. Finally, John Z. had clear reasons that Steve Adams won him over and shared them with the audience.

All said, Rebecca now has an open mind on this candidate because of how clearly and respectfully John made his radio appeal. She took the time to access the *substance* of the appeals, rather than accepting the *surface* information.

Rewind

- Do you find yourself tuning out the news or radio when pundits or commentators are yelling at each other and not respectfully debating an issue?
- How does it make you feel when you are caught in the middle of a heated debate on social media where neither person is listening to the other but rather they're each trying to force the other to accept their point of view?
- Do you ever find yourself getting angry at someone who has a view different from you instead of listening to what they have to say?

[Brief Recap]

Tuning out becomes an immediate response when you don't share an opponent's opinion or perspective. The more they try to convince you that you are wrong, the faster your listening shuts down.

{Tune-in}

It takes patience, discipline, and respect from both sides to listen carefully to other perspectives without immediately tuning out.

8 Mind-Filled Momentum at Work

As a young, ambitious captain in the military, Mark wakes up earlier than his team. His alarm goes off at 4:45 a.m., and he grabs his smartphone from his nightstand to shut off the annoying chirping bird sound.

He sees a few new texts and opens them immediately, almost instinctively. He's already in a bad mood because his girlfriend was texting him late at night complaining that he wasn't available to text her back at midnight.

He gets up with the phone in his hand and checks the device on his wrist to monitor his sleeping patterns. Mark goes to the app, sits back down on his bed, and checks when he was most restless last night.

He notices he has 30 new work e-mails since last night when he spent an extra hour cleaning up his inbox. There's more to check, but he'll get to them later.

Connected While Exercising

Mark gets up and throws on some training gear for an early morning run and workout. His phone and wrist device are with him to track his heart rate, steps, and reps. While he's running, he is listening to a music playlist, also finding a moment to check his texts and scan his e-mail some more.

Because he's not sure how and when to reply to his girlfriend, he starts getting stressed.

By the time he's back home, he grabs breakfast and logs his calories into a nutrition app he's using to help him prepare for an upcoming marathon. While Mark is eating, he looks at some news sites on his laptop, checking a few personal social media sites to see if he's missed anything important from his friends and family.

He finds out that his college roommate was in Las Vegas over the weekend and shared a dozen pictures from a bachelor party. Mark looks at all of them but doesn't recognize any of the guys and starts thinking of fun trips he's had there.

He continues looking at the weather and news. A few more alerts pop up on his phone, but he manages not to open them because he's on a schedule.

Last-Minute Briefing

After he showers and changes, he's headed out the door. It's 6:15 a.m., and he gets a call from his sergeant major saying he's been tasked with leading a briefing after lunch for an important, distinguished visitor. Mark is a last-minute replacement to be the briefer and personal guide for the visiting congressman.

> ► It's so easy to have your mind jump constantly and impulsively from one thought to another as our minds are divided.

Mark quickly Googles the congressman's biography and additional background information. He then forwards some links in a quick e-mail to his second in command to research, then build an agenda, and create a draft slide presentation.

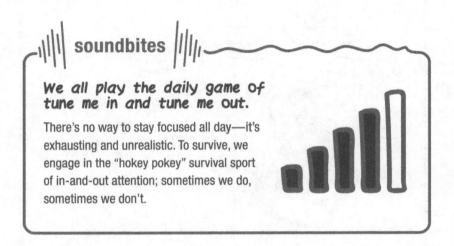

soundbites

We all play the daily game of tune me in and tune me out.

There's no way to stay focused all day—it's exhausting and unrealistic. To survive, we engage in the "hokey pokey" survival sport of in-and-out attention; sometimes we do, sometimes we don't.

Driving Connected

Driving to work, Mark decides to not turn on the radio, but his car automatically detects his phone and continues with his personal playlist. Mark leaves it on, thinking it will give him a chance to relax on his morning commute.

Then his commander calls.

He asks if Mark got his e-mails. Mark is caught off guard and says he hasn't yet. His commander seems frustrated and proceeds to summarize the three e-mails sent last night that he expected would be replied to first thing that morning. The call is short, but Mark thinks he has messed up by missing those messages. He wonders if he should have checked them before he ran.

As he rolls into the office, he sees he has received more e-mails and a few meeting invitations. Mark grabs coffee and logs into his work e-mail that only shares secure communications. There are 20 more e-mail messages there. He quickly scans them and deletes or ignores half of them.

Knowing that he's got to prepare a briefing, he needs to get ready.

Yet More Tasks and E-mails

The commander stops by with a few more tasks. Mark looks up from his computer and takes notes. Now he has to send a few more e-mails to get these new to-dos moving.

Mark has a meeting scheduled midmorning. It's a video teleconference—or VTC—with his counterparts in Europe. It's a weekly call, and he wants to skip it, but he needs to be there for the entire hour while the teams provide updates on their progress and activities. He doesn't see much progress, just lots of busy work, he thinks.

He's stuck in the VTC for more than an hour and has been thinking the entire time how the briefing still isn't complete and his e-mails are still unanswered.

He's frustrated, buried, and behind.

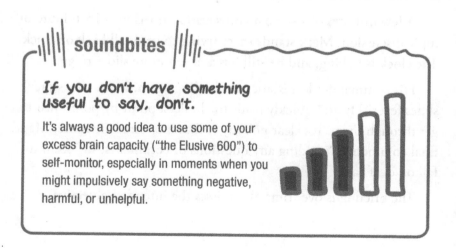

soundbites

If you don't have something useful to say, don't.

It's always a good idea to use some of your excess brain capacity ("the Elusive 600") to self-monitor, especially in moments when you might impulsively say something negative, harmful, or unhelpful.

Heading back to the office, Mark gets stopped by the sergeant major, reminding him to research the distinguished visitor for the briefing. It's lunch and he's glued to his computer, with e-mails half answered and his phone ringing now and then. Most of the calls are minor interruptions, but he can't stop the overflow for more than a few minutes to review his slides for the briefing.

Finally, it's time to greet his guest and deliver the briefing.

There's some pleasant small talk, but Mark isn't even listening that closely because he's worried the slides aren't sufficient, and he hasn't even had a chance to rehearse his delivery. The congressman sits down in the conference room, surrounded by some senior leaders and staff members.

Diving Right into the Weeds

Mark jumps right into the slides, reading the numerous bullet points in the presentation. He's not even two minutes in when the commander stops him and changes the entire direction of the presentation, dwelling on a minor point mentioned a few slides earlier. The congressman follows his lead, they both drill down to the minutiae, and Mark can't get them back on topic.

A few minutes of a sidebar conversation turns into 15-minute off-topic discussion. Mark stands there trying to get it all back on track. The clock is ticking, and he still has a dozen more slides to go.

His commander lets Mark start leading again. Mark clicks the slides feverishly and quickly reads the bullets, point by point, just to get through them. It's clear nobody is that interested anymore. Mark's final comments, "pending any questions or comments, sir" seem to fall on deaf ears.

The briefing is over time and misses the intended objective.

··{ NOTEWORTHY } ·································

The noise leading up to September 11th
Constant chatter and highly fragmented information deafened the listeners

The title of *The 9/11 Commission Report* puts it bluntly: "the system was blinking red."[1] There was an alarming volume of information being reported and collected, coupled with highly fragmented bits of intelligence that generated a steady stream of noise. In the months leading up to that fateful day, most of it was missed.

How could we have overlooked it all?

According to the report, "only a select fraction (of intelligence) can be chosen for briefing the president and senior officials."[2] It became an environment of static that never sounded a clear alarm.

Consider the many warning signs that were buried deep beneath mounds of intelligence:

• Two years earlier, a report by the National Intelligence Council stated that "Al-Qaeda poses the most serious terrorist threat to US security interests," warning that they "could crash-land an aircraft packed with high explosives into the Pentagon, the headquarters of the CIA, or the White House."

• The FAA issued more than a dozen warnings between January and September 11, 2001.

• The FBI, CIA, State Department, and National Security Council all issued repeated threat reports and warnings.

• In June, even the Middle Eastern media network, Al Jazeera, broadcasted videotaped threats against the West from bin Laden.[3]

According to the commission report, there was a spike of chatter that summer pointing to the "high probability of near-term 'spectacular' attacks." All along, Al-Qaeda didn't seem to be hiding its intent, boldly proclaiming a plan to create widespread havoc. One intelligence report tried to raise the urgency by warning that something "very, very, very, very" big was about to happen. Even the use of strong, superlative headlines like "Bin Laden Planning High-Profile Attacks" wasn't enough.[4]

Bottom line: This is noteworthy because we all run the risk of completely missing clear warning signs in our lives when the noise around us reaches deafening levels.

Trying to Salvage Success

As Mark walks the congressman back to his car, he wonders what he could have done differently to improve the interaction. He's worried that his commander and sergeant major will be unhappy with the engagement.

As soon as Mark gets back to his office, his e-mail is already filled with some nasty notes and action items. The noise doesn't stop, and the day drags on.

Mark snaps his fingers, wishing that could make it all go away—it doesn't.

Though not a typical day, Mark feels that he can't keep up and manage the barrage of interruptions, information, and requests. His dream of getting promoted to major seems unrealistic right now. It's a distant dream.

Rewind

- Do you find that you are constantly connected online through-out your day via apps on your phone, text messages, and e-mails?

- Do you feel that it is increasingly difficult to keep up with all of your e-mails and messages, both personal and work-related, and that if you take a break you will miss something?

- Do you exist in an environment in which most of the informa-tion exchanged just sounds like noise, and you feel like tuning everything out?

[Brief Recap]

The constant barrage of information, relentless interruptions, reliance on apps, and constant connection to technology is making it harder than ever to make it through the noisy work day.

{Tune-in}

We can't keep up this pace! The growing, always-on expectation is making work worse.

9 2050: A Parenting Odyssey

L ife seemed much simpler back then.

There's a sense of nostalgia when Emma and Liam recall what life was like when they were growing up 40 years ago. Both were born in 2010 and have fond memories of a much easier life in the decades after the new millennium.

Sitting around the family room one evening, they start to talk about how much life has changed for them. Their two teens, Stephanie and Devin, just roll their eyes and ignore them—some things haven't changed.

The rare family conversation starts because Liam is trying, unsuccessfully, to get his daughter's attention. She is doing homework with her global schoolmates in a virtual immersion classroom. She's been stuck in there for hours.

After failing yet again to get his daughter to unplug and answer his quick question, Liam begins talking out loud. Nobody is listening, but he starts his rant, recalling how his life was so different from theirs. He hears himself sounding like his own parents but doesn't stop his complaints about how tuned in his kids are and how much they're tuning out everyone around them.

His wife Emma hears his complaining and decides to join in.

Technology Was Only a Mild Interrupter for Them

She starts remembering how her own parents would lecture her siblings back in 2025 on how much time they spent on their "smart" phones. She was barely a teen but it was part of their rant.

"Back then, my brothers and sisters were barely connected the way our kids are now. It was all so new. We didn't realize how access to technology would spread so deep and so far into our lives," she quips. "I recall getting started at an early age using connected devices from time to time. Streaming music, social media, texting, and online shopping was just starting to change everything. I couldn't imagine how much further it would complicate our lives as parents."

Her kids' grandparents, she comments, just had tapes and CDs, listened to AM/FM car radio, and watched TV sitcoms every Thursday night back in the 1980s. And kids still drove cars and went to driver's education.

A Carefree Time

For Liam, his stark memory is how his kindergarten class was so innocent and carefree back then.

"None of us pre-K kids had smartphones back then, and we all got driven to school by our parents or a bus driver," he recollects. "The classroom still had books, a few tablets, and even teachers. We actually listened and talked to them and worked on projects with our classmates."

"Paper and printers were still things we used then," his wife chimes in.

How can we spend time with each other when electronic devices have taken over our homes?

Deep Loss of Daily Contact

Both Liam and Emma have almost no real connection with their kids each day. Pervasive technology has inserted itself into every waking—and sleeping—moment of their kids' lives, with almost minimal need for parenting.

Liam and his wife feel like walking paychecks who are meant, seemingly, to finance their kids' daily living. In a world almost completely disconnected from their own, they try to insert themselves, but there's an impermeable bubble around every meaningful moment of contact with their kids. Thinking back, they wonder how much parenting has changed from when they were being raised.

There's little room for even correcting their kids. It's pretty hard to impart wisdom because teens have access to information and advice in almost any imaginable scenario they enter. Cameras and microphones are nearly everywhere. Small talk at dinner is a rarity because activities are so jam packed.

Struggle to Disconnect

Liam and Emma struggle to get their kids away from technology because they need to access it everywhere they go.

"We used to think that not having access to Wi-Fi was our parents' trick, but now every inch of the earth is covered. Our kids laugh when we talk about hotspots and cell phones," Liam observes.

Going on vacation doesn't seem to work either anymore, for a variety of reasons. First, the kids say that they've "experienced" most of it already in virtual reality field trips. Second, they complain that they would have to disconnect and talk to their parents. Finally, they say it's not as fun as their new, virtual worlds.

Technology Is with You Everywhere You Go

As Devin walks by his parents, he senses that their conversation might be uncomfortable for him, so he turns his head quickly, blinks a few times into his glasses and starts a quick video session.

His dad notices but doesn't want to start a fight by correcting his son yet again.

"We had technology but we didn't wear it in everything. We carried phones but now that's all on and around them. Some people even surgically implant it," Liam comments.

It's Just Living for Them

Devin and Stephanie have plenty of reason to make fun of how far technology has come since their parents were young. They don't even consider using terms like *the Internet* and *technology;* it's just living. They laugh about the obsessions with smartphones, since cameras, sensors, and connectivity are common devices throughout every corner of society.

They laugh at how much their parents' generation, back in 2020, obsessed with the next model smartphone, texting, and social networking because now nobody needs them. There are now screens and sensors everywhere that recognize you at any moment.

"You can't get them off because they're always on," Emma says. "It's like breathing for them."

Why Did We Worry So Much?

"I had friends of mine text girls if they wanted to go to the dance with me. It was pretty hard work reminding them to help me out," Liam recalls. "Their dating now requires no effort at all. I had to make a plan, but now all of that is paired automatically. It's like the prearranged marriage centuries ago, but now an algorithm does the matching, not their parents."

As Liam is lamenting his painstaking dating woes, his wife needs to catch herself from laughing herself to tears. On the way to her first high school dance, all the parents would get together to take the same awkward pictures, taking out their "smart" phones and sharing them online with one another afterwards. Even the limo driver waited impatiently because they all were basically taking the same shots.

It all seems so old-fashioned now, as their kids are all driven by autonomous cars and photos and videos are constantly being taken of them—not by them—wherever they go.

"I remember some of my friends having to drive themselves to school and sports and how their parents told them not to check their phones as they were driving," Emma said. "Our parents actually bought us used cars and worried about us texting and driving. It doesn't seem possible now that the kids get picked up and dropped off anywhere in a moment's notice. All cars are autonomous, on a subscription, connected to everything so there's no worry of distracted accidents anymore."

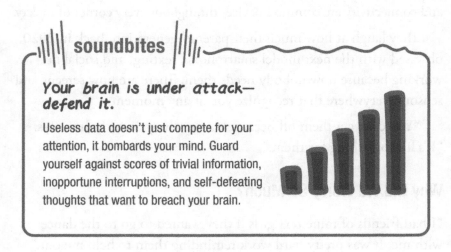

soundbites

Your *brain* is under *attack*—defend it.

Useless data doesn't just compete for your attention, it bombards your mind. Guard yourself against scores of trivial information, inopportune interruptions, and self-defeating thoughts that want to breach your brain.

Parenting without a Voice

As Liam and Emma are sharing these funny and sad memories, their kids aren't hearing a word. Liam and Emma can't change that now.

Devin and Stephanie are basically out of reach from them during the day, constantly dialed in to music, friends, and artificial living.

"If they didn't have to eat, we might never see them," he complains. "It's impossible talking to them when they're gone all the time and get their learning from everything else but us. We are constantly trying to find a way back in, but it's tough to be more engaging than all the other exciting stuff that they have access to. Parents have never seemed so boring and irrelevant."

Fighting a Force

Emma steps in and emotionally recollects about how her parents used to punish her, give her chores and unsolicited advice. She and Liam even crave more of this time and interaction with their kids, yet they always seem to be fighting a force that was slowly developing and taking over during their childhood years.

"We all were so enamored with the emerging world of the Internet, devices, and connectivity back then," she says. "I guess we didn't realize just how addicting and pervasive it would all become for our kids and for us. None of us saw it coming, and we weren't aware of how it all wasn't going to slow down."

Rewind

- Take a moment to think about the future and our use of technology. If you feel like you're always connected now, how might that look 20 years down the line?

- If you're a parent, do you notice that your kids are always tuned into their devices? Has it changed the way you communicate with them as opposed to how your parents communicated with you?

- Do you notice yourself communicating less face-to-face with family members and friends and having most of your conversations digitally?

- How have digital distractions decreased your family dynamics?

[Brief Recap]

Parents in the future will have to compete for their child's attention with always-on connectivity. Virtual reality and other technologies may become a threat to the family structure and undermine existing family roles and interactions.

{Tune-in}

We need to monitor the use of pervasive technology. If unchecked, it can become addictive and isolating, weakening the family and personal relationships.

10 Safety Briefing with Near-Tragic Results

T he passengers were stunned, engulfed in a cloud of smoke and steady rain.

Their aircraft lay partially charred in a field next to a small lake, careening off the runway after an emergency landing. An engine fire and landing gear incident—a rare double episode—caused their flight to make a forced landing, in a storm, at a small, rural airport with a short runway.

"It's a miracle all the passengers didn't die," said a first responder. "There was such confusion. Nobody did what they were supposed to do."

The looming issue for many years that passengers were ignoring the preflight safety briefing finally came true. Research had predicted it was going to happen: a majority of people admit they regularly tune out the safety briefing as a preflight annoyance.[1] Recognizing the hidden risks, the airline industry had tried everything—celebrities, comedy, and even technical explanations—yet it all was continuously ignored.

In a trance

► We're so glued to digital devices that
we don't see the risks ahead.

As the plane was flying over bad weather at 37,000 feet, an engine exploded in flames, ripping a hole in the fuselage. The plane immediately lost cabin pressure, exposing the passengers to subzero temperatures and oxygen-depleted air. As the breathing masks deployed, many of the passengers didn't know how to use them at all. Wearing seatbelts saved those near the growing hole near a window, many of whom were nearly sucked out.

It was later reported that a few dozen digital devices went flying out that hole in an instant.

As the plane rapidly descended through turbulent weather, the flight crew looked for a nearby airport to land. Inside the cabin, chaos ensued. Passengers panicked. The flight attendants tried to calm them but were ignored. Hypoxia, or the lack of oxygen to the brain, posed a fatal threat if the masks weren't put on quickly.

The turbulence and lightning sparked panic.

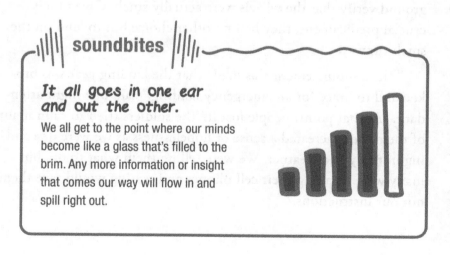

soundbites

It all goes in one ear and out the other.
We all get to the point where our minds become like a glass that's filled to the brim. Any more information or insight that comes our way will flow in and spill right out.

"The safety announcements were ignored, and many of the passengers weren't putting on their masks at all or were doing it wrong," one observer said. "They were screaming, yelling at the flight attendants, and trying to connect their phones and laptops to send off a message."

In the confusion, a group of retired military reservists returning from a convention responded. They started going through the cabin, securing people's masks properly and forcing others to turn their phones off and listen.

"It was a moment to force some immediate training on them," one soldier said.

As the plane descended over the next 15 minutes, approaching the small-town airport, the problems in the cockpit were just growing. In the flight deck, the crew discovered, to their surprise, that the landing gear wasn't working. Under normal circumstances, they would fly over the runway to have emergency crews on the ground verify that the wheels were actually stuck. Given their crucial predicament, they had no other choice but to land on the small runway.

"The announcement was made that the landing gear was broken and to brace for an emergency landing," said one flight attendant. "At that point, people lost it. The soldiers tried to calm many of them, but it created a sense of hopelessness as we were descending in really bad weather. We were telling them what to do, but many were thinking their cell phones and texting would save them, not our instructions."

··{ NOTEWORTHY } ··

Listen up, I might die
A training session where the vital part was missed

Technical training can be painful, tedious, and boring. Too many details, poor preparation, and weak instructors are certainly key contributors.

One afternoon, I was leading a BRIEF 101 course for some soldiers, and we started to discuss the topic of training. Specifically, we were trying to brainstorm what we might do to liven it up, simplify it, and make it less awful. It turns out that a majority of military training seems to be pretty sub-par.

During the open discussion, one of the guys just chimed in.

"I remember being in this one predeployment training brief," he said without expression. "I distinctly remember thinking and saying to myself in a specific moment, 'Hey, you need to listen to what this guy's saying because if you don't, you might get killed.' And a few seconds later, I realized I had zoned out completely and didn't hear a single word the instructor said. I missed it all."

The guys in the class erupted in laughter, either confirming they had a similar experience or maybe surprised it was a miracle that he hadn't died due to distraction.

His story stopped me in my tracks. How could it be that even with something that would save your life, you still might miss it by not fully listening? Imagine if you weren't paying attention at all—that's bad enough. But in this case, he knew his attention to all of the details was crucial, yet they still went in one ear and out the other.

Bottom line: This story is noteworthy because we are naïve to think that people will always be able to listen to and truly hear critical information.

The landing was really hard.

The damaged plane raced quickly along the runway, with flames all around, as panic grew. Miraculously, the aircraft didn't break apart. As it roared to a stop, well beyond the runway into a field near a lake, most passengers jumped to evacuate.

"People didn't follow directions at all," the flight attendant continued. "They got up and started grabbing their carry-ons and clawing for the door. It was a traffic jam and nearly impossible to get them out because people were confused about where the right exit doors were."

As the plane started to fill with smoke, the reservists stepped in to force order and get people to listen. Together with the three flight attendants, the dozen retired soldiers marshaled the entire cabin to safety. As the local emergency crew put out most of the fire, the steady rain did the rest.

"It was amazing that nobody was hurt," said one soldier. "It was like nobody on the plane even took time to pay attention to a safety briefing. There was mass ignorance, and it was scary to watch people grab their bags and put everyone at harm."

Rewind

- Do you notice yourselves and others tuning out during safety briefings? How could this affect you in the case of an emergency?
- Do you examine your surroundings when in a plane, train, or other crowded area and have a plan of action, if needed?
- Reflect on how our loss of focus is putting us more at risk.

[Brief Recap]

Daydreaming, spacing out, becoming distracted, or assuming information is irrelevant is a dangerous habit that might impact a career, a promotion, or a life.

{Tune-in}

We need to self-monitor our listening habits because the attitude of "I've heard it all before" can have devastating consequences.

Part Three

Time for You to Tune In: Awareness Management (AM 101)

11 Awareness Management 101

Managing awareness is a personal responsibility. "Keep your head in the game," as the expression goes, needs to be something we do intentionally. After all, as our thoughts start wandering off, it's really our minds that are adrift.

It's easy for people to have hours—and perhaps days—go by as if they're not mentally there at all. For example, you're driving to work and you can't remember a single turn or traffic pattern; you just sat in an hour-long meeting but what happened is a total blur; you're involved in a conversation, but you find you're not listening at all but wondering if your favorite team is playing tonight; after swiping your smartphone for hours at a time, you have practically no recollection of what you've read, viewed, or played.

Awareness can be a seemingly easy concept to grasp but a tough term to define. Because it is often used synonymously with terms like focus, knowledge, mindfulness, alertness, enlightenment, perception, consciousness, and understanding, it can be easily diluted and misunderstood.

Lighting the Path Before Us

As discussed earlier, your attention is a precious and scarce commodity that can be easily depleted.

According to Templafy, a technology provider, the average office worker receives 121 e-mails per day and sends 40 business e-mails a day.[1] These continual interruptions drain our brain. Think of it as a mental fuel tank that can go empty. If your mind is all over the place, it's similar to driving a car until it runs out of gas.

In essence, awareness management is a conscious command of one's attention. It's directing the mind like a flashlight on an object that's surrounded by shadows, dim light, and darkness.

When it's obscure, we might miss what's in front of us. But when it's fully illuminated and directed, we can see things clearly. So, consider awareness like a hiker's headlamp, pointing the light on a trail so the hiker can navigate the path confidently.

In a nutshell, awareness management means the more intentional the hiker's headlamp, the more directed the light.

According to Daniel Goleman, author of *Focus: The Hidden Driver of Excellence*, "Active engagement of attention signifies top-down (brain) activity, an antidote to going through the day with a zombie-like automaticity. We can talk back to commercials, stay alert to what's happening around us, question automatic routines and what improves them. This focused, often goal-oriented attention, inhibits mindless mental habits."[2]

Lives Can Become a Blur

Those mindless moments can turn into days and then become weeks, months, and even years for some people. The risk is that we become a passenger in the car of our own life—with nobody at the wheel.

Where am I going? What am I doing? What was I thinking?

I recall when, many years ago, Tom, both a client and friend of mine, recounted his days as a serious drug addict. Although he recovered with help from friends and overcame many obstacles along the way, his past was pretty dark.

During a conversation one day, I asked him what it was like to be an addict and to live, as he did, under a bridge in Miami. His life, currently a modern-day success story, stood in stark contrast to his serious addictions. I asked him how he survived it all.

"Barely," he said. "One time, I went on a trip through Latin America for a month. I ended up on a beach somewhere, and I don't remember a single thing."

To this day, when I think of Tom and how our lives can become a blur, I ponder what it is like for people who are that generally unaware. They are there, but not *really* there.

Missing the Moment Entirely

Tom's vague recollections, although caused by serious addictions, can point us to similar, unnoticed risks: missing moments—or a life—entirely. We frequently overlook this threat when we race mindlessly from one thing to another. It may be half-listening to our kids, dismissing the cues of a co-worker or customer, or avoiding critical details to make an important decision.

We move through moments yet are not really living them. Being able to focus more intentionally and purposefully means thriving more in these moments, creating more meaningful memories, and being more productive, impactful, and complete.

Years later, my friend Tom was trying to capture those blurry, lost years. Many of us might be so addicted to our own distractions that we may face a similar fate.

Our Minds Are Spinning Beach Balls

Our attention is an expendable, scarce resource.

There's a serious energy cost to the misuse of the brain's gas tank. Even the term "paying attention" implies a transaction that depletes an account. Given the vast number of distractions around us, we must intentionally protect and preserve our attention balance from morning to night.

At my office, we often joke about the "beach ball," that spinning icon on a computer that indicates the processor is running but nothing much is happening. Think of your misused attention as the spinning wheel that's trying to process but just keeps spinning.

Imagine if you start your day and exhaust high-quality attention on consuming pointless information and thinking useless thoughts. You've already wasted valuable energy during your morning routine by jumping between reading news feeds, checking social media, looking at the weather in a city in which you don't live, and deleting scores of e-mails.

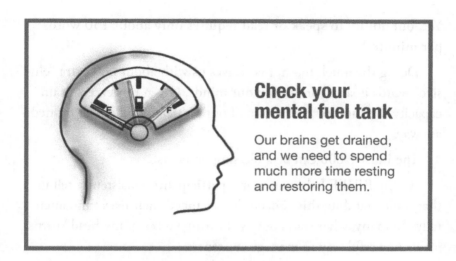

Check your mental fuel tank

Our brains get drained, and we need to spend much more time resting and restoring them.

Every ounce of attention you lose in these precious moments weakens your ability to effectively perform in your first meeting and to manage the difficult daily tasks that demand real concentration. As you tackle these duties, you feel your mind drift back toward what the brain craves, which is jumping between more "mindless" activities.

Multitasking is a prevalent problem.

According to Udemy Research, 70% of people feel distracted while working, with 16% admitting to being almost always distracted. Thirty-six percent of Millennials and Gen Z-ers say they spend more than two hours of their workday on social media.[3]

This makes it hard to keep your head in the game.

The Elusive 600: Your Enemy or Your Friend?

As you know by now, the brain is a great processor. Some research estimates indicate that the brain can process about 750 words per minute.

Yet, our ability to speak or read requires only about 150 words per minute.[4]

Doing the quick math, that leaves us with about 600 extra "elusive" words floating around in our minds. Given this excess brain capacity, we can become "aware of our awareness" in a real, immediate way.

The Elusive 600 can be a blessing or a curse.

At The BRIEF Lab, our course participants consistently tell us that understanding this concept has changed their lives fundamentally. To many, what starts out as "hearing voices in my head" turns into a powerful way to manage awareness.

In essence, being aware of the Elusive 600 serves as a means to self-monitor, using excess capacity productively to recognize impulsive responses, gauge disinterest, and moderate errant thoughts and comments throughout the day.

It's as if you are having an ongoing conversation with your brain.

Runaway Thoughts

When it goes unchecked, the Elusive 600 is like letting a squirrel free in your attic. It runs around, wreaking havoc. You have no way to capture and control it.

Here are a few errant thoughts that might be running around upstairs in your head, in need of monitoring:

I have a point to add to this discussion. Wait, maybe I should hear her out and just listen.

I wonder what e-mails have come since this meeting began? Wait, I should pay attention to what's going on. I can check e-mail later.

What's this speaker's intention? Wait, I need to be objective and patient.

What's for dinner? Wait, that has nothing to do with this meeting.

I have seven things to do. Wait, my shoe is untied.

When is he going to finish this paragraph and change topics? Wait, he may have another good story to add.

Waking Your Mind from Mindlessness to Mindfulness

Much has been said about mindfulness. It's a term that has swept away business leaders, celebrities, and common folk with force and fury.

Though I feel strongly that much of the movement may fade as overblown fads often do, I'm convinced that the fundamental need to be more "aware of our awareness"—and to actively do something about it—will remain.

The issue is avoiding the mindless waste of mental energy and moving toward the conservation and preservation of concentration. We need to consider both the quantity and quality of our attention.

Where and how can we start to wake up and manage our awareness? Like trying to wake from a deep sleep, the best way to be more alert is to sound an awareness alarm in a few core areas of your life that may often feel flat or seriously underinflated:

- **Relationships:** Do I know people around me well or are my relationships pretty superficial?

- **Reputation:** Am I known as a person who gets the job done, or do I jump around from one task to another and another, reaching few goals?

- **Productivity:** Do the things I spend my time on matter or are they trivial? Do they waste my energy and generate few results?

This wake-up call—gaining *an awareness of our awareness*—makes us more willful, purposeful, and intentional. Letting our minds go into "screensaver" mode has us walking through life, never really present to what's happening.

Directed, Undirected, and Misdirected

The expression "pay attention" makes sense as we dive deeper into where and how our minds concentrate.

There are different types of attention.

- Our choice to concentrate is *directed attention.*

- Our intentional move to let our minds wander is *undirected attention.*

- Our less productive, more troublesome use of the brain is wasted energy, or *misdirected attention.*

Here are a few simple ways to better understand each type of attention:		
DIRECTED ATTENTION	**UNDIRECTED ATTENTION**	**MISDIRECTED ATTENTION**
Intentionally focusing	Purposeful mind-wandering	Permitting distractions
EXAMPLE		
Looking out an airplane window to determine your location	Looking out an airplane window at all the clouds and ground below	Looking out an airplane window and worrying if there might be unexpected turbulence
ANALOGY		
Turning on a lamp at night to read	Leaving on a night-light in case you wake up in the middle of the night	Leaving all your house lights on when there's nobody home
RISK/REWARD		
You can clearly read your surroundings	You might relax and be ready for inspiration	You waste time and energy with little gain

Daniel Goleman's book on improving focus also explores the steady battle that goes on between our awareness and our distractions. "At the neural level, mind wandering and perceptual awareness tend to inhibit each other: internal focus on our train of thought tunes out the senses, while being rapt in the beauty of a sunset quiets the mind. This tune-out can be total, as when we get utterly lost in what we're doing."[5]

This battle can hinder the benefits of wonder, so we should let our mind do what it does best and allow these positive attention habits.

Commit to "Awareness Management"

Think of all of the critical activities in business that include the word "management."

For example, human resources management deals with people, supply chain management with logistics and vendors, and crisis management with unexpected incidents and risks. These, along with many other areas of business, require specialized management skills to handle diverse demands.

In all these areas, we dedicate time, resources, and attention to guide activities toward a positive end. Awareness management belongs on the top of this list, so we can succeed personally and professionally.

There's much to gain—and lose—if this valuable resource is squandered.

···{ NOTEWORTHY } ·····································

Engineering mindfulness: A systematic approach
Preparing university students to be more purposeful and intentional

When Northwestern University professor Joe Holtgreive began teaching engineering students over 20 years ago, he noticed how ineffective they were at handling problem-solving during moments of peak stress. Their academic and professional success depended largely upon how mindful they were and how they managed their attention in these difficult moments.

"It became clearer and clearer to me over the years the role attention played in those moments of intense uncertainty," he said.

Holtgreive strongly contends that engineers tend to be bright people who have been celebrated for their analytical ability to solve difficult, complex problems. Yet they are still human beings with emotional and intuitive minds that can work against them in stressful situations. Natural reactions to stress can cause them to lose focus and make mistakes.

His inspired idea was to train them to be not just successful engineers but also successful problem-solvers under stress. He and the university created the Engineering Office of Personal Development (EOPD), which teaches students "engineering mindfulness."

He describes "engineering mindfulness" as a quality of attention necessary for living in the moment. His intention was to create an office that established different mechanisms and structures to help students develop these critical skills.

He and his colleagues give students the tools to let go of their urge to "freeze up" when overwhelmed by the difficulty and urgency of a problem and, instead, let distractions fall away to focus on the problem at hand. The EOPD curriculum consists of workshops that feature thought leaders and courses whose content includes emotional intelligence, mindfulness, and even dancing and improv comedy techniques.

"The present moment is the only opportunity we get to show up for our lives, and how we show up matters," he says. "It's an honor and privilege to help students recognize the power they have in these moments."

Bottom line: This program is noteworthy because it has created "whole-being" engineers who are ready to bring their entire selves mindfully into each moment.

What If We Don't Manage Our Awareness?

I have often succumbed to noise that depleted my attention. Maybe it was hours online, obsessing over an errant comment someone made, or wasting energy worrying about things that didn't amount to anything.

Regardless, I paid a price when I didn't manage my awareness.

Here's my "distraction risk list," featuring the effects we experience when we thoughtlessly tune into the noise around us:

- Wasted time
- Needless worry
- No focus
- Missed clues
- Confusion
- Poor decisions
- Impulsiveness
- Delayed response
- Mental fatigue
- Lack of vision

The risk list can grow even longer. Take time to reflect on the impact you face if you don't habitually manage where your mind is throughout the day.

What do you gain by letting yourself tune in to so much noise? As mentioned in an earlier chapter, when we consume useless noise it's like we are consuming "brain celery," those empty calories that make us mentally anemic.

If we don't think, our brains weaken.

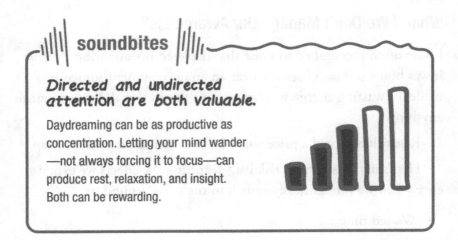

soundbites

Directed and undirected attention are both valuable.

Daydreaming can be as productive as concentration. Letting your mind wander —not always forcing it to focus—can produce rest, relaxation, and insight. Both can be rewarding.

AM Pre-set Buttons

Just like a radio dial, we can create pre-set buttons to make managing our awareness a daily practice.

Here are some practical ways that I will set out in the upcoming chapters to help you learn to become a master of Awareness Management:

1. Set your sights on what's essential.

2. Say no.

3. Embrace quiet time.

4. Give the gift of present listening.

Rewind

- Are you aware whether you check your e-mail, news, and social media on your smartphone the first thing in the morning before you even get out of bed?
- Do you feel like your mind automatically wanders and weakens when thinking about things that really don't matter much?
- Are there moments in your daily life that can be managed more intentionally and purposefully to help hone your focus?

[Brief Recap]

By becoming more aware of our awareness, moment to moment, we can avoid useless or unproductive distractions and clearly focus on the task in front of us. We need to grasp the negative impact that unintentional, automatic mindlessness has on our brains. We need to give our minds time to intentionally drift to discover and uncover new ideas, emotions, and connections.

{Tune-in}

Practice managing your awareness and avoiding thoughts and actions that deplete your brain.

12 Take Aim: Set Your Sights on What Matters Most

In this chapter, the word "most" is what I want you to embrace. What is the *most* important thing right now? Not what is *more* important between many choices, but what's the *most* valuable—the top, highest, maximum, chief, greatest, uppermost. You get the point; that is where we all need to take precise aim.

In the infamous words of Yogi Berra, "If you don't know where you're going, you might not get there." Consider that funny line and start to carefully consider how you set your priorities at work or at home.

Do you know your priorities? Are they effective? Are there things you'd like to accomplish but never seem to get to? Do you find distractions derail you, or do you notice at all?

For many of us, it's similar to setting out on a journey without determining a specific destination (i.e. an address, a hotel, a landmark, etc.). In your mind, you're just headed in a general direction.

Retracing your steps later, you see how you were all over the road, wasting energy and time along the way. In our age of infobesity and interruptions, our lives can meander in wild twists and turns. Many times, we may not even notice we do this at all.

We won't get very far unless we take aim at what matters most.

Essentialists versus Non-essentialists

In his remarkable book *Essentialism*, Greg McKeown sets out powerful ways to avoid the burden of excess by embracing fewer things in your daily life. He challenges people to become essentialists. Those burdened by excess are non-essentialists.

An essentialist chooses to focus on a few, vital things, and a non-essentialist has someone or something else set their priorities and chases many things.

The side-by-side comparison is stark:

ESSENTIALIST	NON-ESSENTIALIST
Less	More
Discipline	Chaos
Concise	Long-winded
Says "no" often	Says "yes" to everything
Sharpshooter	Shotgun
Certainty	Confusion
Finds silence	Filled with noise

McKeown is realistic in his message. "It's not just the number of choices that has increased exponentially, it is also the strength and number of outside influences on our decisions that has increased."[1]

No More Deafening Noise

Our lives can become flooded with more and more stuff. Moment to moment, our minds are crammed to the brim—like closets, basements, and bedrooms in a hoarder's house—teeming with useless, trivial information and ongoing diversions that seem important in the moment and prove to be of little value later on.

What's more, we have so many choices to make. Go online to rent a movie and there are thousands and thousands to consider. Head to the grocery store and look for pasta and sauce; there are dozens. Look for games in the app store and you can wander for hours looking at an endless list of options. Most of it is overwhelming and confusing, especially if we don't have a filter to determine what's right versus what's to be avoided.

A techdirt.com article on video streaming brings attention to our abundance of choices, "Nearly half (47%) of US consumers say they're frustrated by the growing number of subscriptions and services required to watch what they want, according to the thirteenth edition of Deloitte's annual Digital Media Trends survey. 'Consumers want choice—but only up to a point,' said Kevin Westcott, Deloitte vice chairman and US telecom and media and entertainment leader, who oversees the study. 'We may be entering a time of "subscription fatigue."'"[2]

We feel the steady loss of energy and time, like water pouring through our fingers. Everything that beckons for our attention seems vital, yet very few things are vitalizing. As the noise levels increase, our daily lives don't feel much like living. Instead we feel we are just spinning in place.

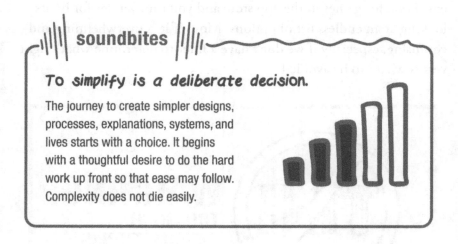

soundbites

To simplify is a deliberate decision.

The journey to create simpler designs, processes, explanations, systems, and lives starts with a choice. It begins with a thoughtful desire to do the hard work up front so that ease may follow. Complexity does not die easily.

Pointless Routines

For one midlevel manager and father of two, it took hitting the wall one day to admit the pointlessness of his busy, futile, daily routines.

Every morning Steve would wake up and immediately check his smartphone. He'd scan multiple e-mail accounts, check weather, stocks, news feeds, social media, and sports. He navigated his smartphone like a Swiss Army knife, clicking and swiping from place to place in nanoseconds.

In a matter of moments, his brain was humming. It carried on through the commute, into meetings, and on the way home.

When he'd walk in the door at home, he was agitated and couldn't focus. Family life didn't move the same way. He couldn't settle down to patiently talk with his wife and complained in his head that she should get to the point faster.

While helping his kids with their homework, an internal battle waged as he tried to focus on teaching them as he checked his phone for updates, e-mails, and social media. This routine of self-induced distractions, constant multitasking, and dispersive attention became his new normal.

Then Steve and his family went on a weeklong vacation to the mountains. They were so far away from the big city that technology not only didn't work, it also seemed out of place in that beautiful environment.

Fast-forward seven days. He returned from vacation happy, calm, and centered. He no longer wanted to be the proverbial hamster on the spinning wheel and began to limit his time checking his phone.

Steve's family and co-workers started to notice he was a different person. He was a better listener, he slowed down more, he was getting things done, and he was present in the moment.

A Minimalist Decision: Keep It Simple

There's wisdom in the adage "less is more."

In an era of supersaturation and excessive choices, our options can quickly overwhelm and permanently paralyze us. It's not just daily media usage and technology access, but the vast array of possible alternatives from investments, clothing, colleges, salad dressings, strategies, and vacation spots. According to Alina Tugend, in a *New York Times* article about the paralyzing effect of facing too many choices, "An excess of choices often leads us to be less, not more, satisfied once we actually decide. There is often that nagging feeling we could have done better."[3]

Decision-making has never been harder, and our focus has never been more strained.

Too many choices

Endless options are a great source of noise in our lives. Whether it's groceries, online movies, streaming music, cars, or flights, our mind gets overwhelmed looking for the perfect choice.

General Bernard Montgomery, a primary architect of the D-Day invasion, drafted a one-page, hand-written directive to orchestrate the movement of more than 156,000 troops on June 6, 1944. At the bottom of the directive, he wrote the word "simplicity," and underlined it three times.

Simplicity was the key to the invasion's success. The single-minded focus of the commanders and the troops in the midst of that highly complex operation was remarkable.

A minimalist movement has taken root in our culture, providing fewer moving parts to run our lives. Millennials have quickly embraced this movement.

We're more than overdue, since in the United States today, as mentioned by becomingminimalist.com, most homes have more televisions than residents, and we consume 50% more material goods than just 50 years ago.[4]

··{ NOTEWORTHY } ··

Marie Kondo and the Kon-Mari Method
An organizational guru sparks joy

Who doesn't love—or perhaps dread—a good spring cleaning? It is a great time to start anew, to clear out the cobwebs, reduce clutter, and possibly gain a calmer mind.

This is why Marie Kondo's book,*The Life-Changing Magic of Tidying Up: The Japanese Art of Decluttering and Organizing*, has had a worldwide impact, where it became a *New York Times* best-seller and sold millions of copies.

People are definitely looking for guidance in cleaning up their lives. They've had enough of clutter.

Kondo's approach—the Kon-Mari Method—is "Start by discarding. Then organize your space, thoroughly, completely, in one go." By "taking each item in your hand, asking yourself whether it sparks joy, and deciding on this basis whether or not to keep it," Kondo's mission is to "spark joy" in the world through tidying, as she believes most people have way too much stuff, and letting go is even more important than adding.

Her suggestions don't just produce organized drawers, but a more balanced life, as she observes, "Life becomes far easier once you know that things will still work out even if you are lacking something," suggesting that tidying gives you more confidence to make better decisions.

Certainly, we are seeing that impulsivity, convenience, and affordability create the perfect storm to easily and unknowingly hoard so many things that we wake up to find our lives filled to the brim with items that weigh us down, not lift us up.

What's more, the same conditions can create similar chaos in our already jam-packed minds. We need to clean up our psychological space just as we clean up our physical ones.

Bottom line: Marie Kondo's best-selling book is noteworthy because the effect of decluttering your space goes hand-in-hand with reducing the noise in your head and all around you.

Aim Small, Miss Small—Tips to Direct Your Focus

In the Army, snipers are a breed apart. They train extensively to achieve high levels of concentration, patience, and precision. Those whom I have met are remarkable professionals and terrific human beings, each with a willingness to share aspects of their craft openly. One of their mantras is "Aim small, miss small."

This means that when they select a target in their scope, they intentionally focus on an even smaller part of the object (e.g. an edge, a button, a small part of an item). The basic idea is that if you miss by a few centimeters, you will still hit the target.

The same is true with taking aim in our daily activities and routines. We need similar discipline.

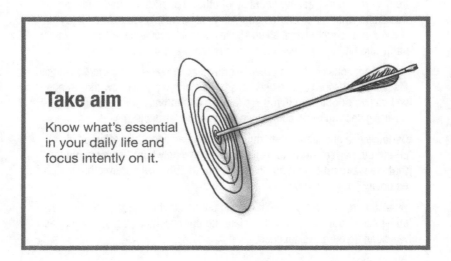

Take aim

Know what's essential
in your daily life and
focus intently on it.

Here are five specific ideas to help you take aim and prioritize a few essential things in your life. I've included additional insights that address potential objections, actions, and results (think of them like OAR, for short, to keep you "rowing" in the right direction).

- **Idea 1: A step forward: a silent retreat.** Consider how moments of quiet contemplation can provide the peace and serenity we need to go deeper to define what matters most for each of us. In my own circles, I'm encouraged to go on an annual retreat. Every year, I resist. It is three days of silence that seem unbearable on Friday but a gift once I'm finished on Sunday afternoon. During that time, I set bigger goals, assess lifelong dreams, and reset myself while in prayerful contemplation.

- ◆ **Objections:** I'm busy; I'll do it later; it won't work for me.
- ◆ **Actions:** Schedule time away; do a turn-it-all-off weekend; wake up an hour earlier with no technology access.
- ◆ **Result:** Listen to what you hear; get some rest; feel at peace.

- **Idea 2: Write it down.** After telling one of his corny jokes, the infamous Irish comedian Hal Roach used to say, "Write it down! Write it down!" Lest we forget, it's critical to jot down our "north star" goals. David Allen, productivity speaker and author of *Getting Things Done,* says writing things down can help you capture and clarify what is important and what can be discarded.

  - ◆ **Objections:** It's just going to change again tomorrow; my boss or significant other sets my agenda, not me; I like to keep my options open.

  - ◆ **Actions:** Get a coach or advisor to help you set a vision; buy a pack of Post-It Notes, frame your big goal, and post it somewhere that you will see often.

  - ◆ **Result:** Making a decision to set a specific course will empower and direct you.

- **Idea 3: Make a private, then public pact.** As social beings, setting priorities transcends us personally. Our goals and dreams affect us, as well as others, in countless ways. Our co-workers, friends, kids, and clients all feel a difference when we focus on fewer things with greater intensity and purpose. That said, we need to share our plan to simplify our lives. After all, they're not mind readers.

- ♦ **Objections:** If I change my plans, I will lose credibility; it's a personal matter; I don't feel comfortable sharing.
- ♦ **Actions:** Make a short list of "safe" people with whom to share your plan; schedule time to declare your objectives to them; ask others to spread the word.
- ♦ **Result:** People around you can help keep you accountable and support you.
- **Idea 4: Keep it in the galaxy—in time and space.** Setting a "north star" should not be a far-off, distant dream. We make our vision real by keeping our feet planted on earth and making time and space for it. This means moving schedules around and removing obstacles that impede our progress.
  - ♦ **Objections:** I'm not a good planner; my schedule changes moment to moment; my willpower is weak.
  - ♦ **Actions:** Read the book *Getting Things Done* by David Allen; review your calendar and block off time; create a physical space at work or home to reflect on your progress.
  - ♦ **Result:** Developing a stronger sense of realism and willfulness.
- **Idea 5: Throw away something.** Find an item that you don't use and don't need and throw it in the trash. Clutter comes in many forms. You need to develop the habit and willpower to rid yourself of these excesses. They won't stand up and leave on their own.
  - ♦ **Objections:** I might need it someday; that seems drastic; I paid good money for it.
  - ♦ **Actions:** Find a shirt or pair of shoes you don't wear and give them to charity. Delete an app on your phone you haven't used in the past six months.
  - ♦ **Result:** Uncluttering your world will encourage more minimalism.

Post It: Simplicity Isn't Complicated

As Ronald Reagan once said, "There are no easy answers, but there are simple answers." Our tendency is to complicate our daily lives much more than they need to be. I certainly do this, and maybe you do, too.

There's far too much to juggle in our lives: professional life, home life, finances, technology, religion, activities, expectations, cars, entertainment, hobbies, gossip, exercise, shopping, apps, news, food, threats, drama, events, deadlines, commutes, meetings, healthcare, image, sports, music. The list is long and the likelihood for complexity and complication is great.

What really matters? It's not 50 things. It's maybe 5—and should be fewer.

It helps me if I write my defining "go-to" goals in a few words on a small Post-It note. I put it on my desk or on a bathroom mirror as a visible reminder, and I remove all the clutter around it.

These Post-It notes force me to keep my goals simple. It's not a list. It sits there stuck to my desk, my refrigerator, or in my bathroom, unpretentiously telling me what I've decided really matters.

That's it. Bam! Three words ("write next book"); two words ("listen more"); four words from the Chicago Cubs ("try not to suck").

You get the point.

To Simplify Is a Deliberate Decision

Mindfulness expert John Kabat-Zinn once advised, "Voluntary simplicity means going fewer places in one day than more, seeing less so I can see more, doing less so I can do more, acquiring less so I can have more."[5]

There's much to be gained by managing fewer moving parts.

Think of your life like a machine—the more components, the greater the possibility of something breaking and needing repair.

One of the best bits of advice on this topic comes from a small book, *The Elements of Style*. In it, the authors Will Strunk and E.B. White provide practical ways to improve writing. Their three-word gem inspired me to write my book BRIEF:

"Omit needless words" (point #17).

"A sentence should contain no unnecessary words, a paragraph no unnecessary sentences, for the same reason that a drawing should have no unnecessary lines and a machine no unnecessary parts."[6]

Brilliant advice.

In our lives, only a few things are necessary.

The paradox is we have to give something away to get something in return. Are we givers or takers? Are we filling our lives with excess stuff—hanging on to an old pair of boots, an extra word in a pointless meeting, more clicks and swipes on our phone, or giving into another tempting distraction?

Like the song in the Disney animation film *Frozen* exclaims, "Let it go, let it go, let it go!"

Rewind

- Consider your priorities for your work or your life. How many are there? Does your list seem overwhelming? Does it lack focus?
- What actions can you take today to simplify your life?
- Which of the suggestions outlined in this chapter could you adopt today?

[Brief Recap]

When we keep things simple in life we are more focused, productive, and present. When we don't, we feel a heavy burden that weighs us down and makes us wander slowly.

{Tune-in}

Set your sights on fewer priorities, not more activities, choices, and stuff.

13 Saying No to Noise

There's a famous saying, "There is no 'I' in 'team.'" Now think about the word "noise." There's not only an "I" in it, but also an "n" and an "o."

Is this pure coincidence or a sign? You decide.

"No" is a powerful little word. It can stop bad decisions, sudden impulses, unwanted offers, and debilitating tendencies. It is as unambiguous as it is direct.

Hear its power…

No, thank you!

No more for me

No money in the account

No time on the clock

No excuses

No clue

No ifs, ands, or buts

No pain, no gain

Just Say No

In the late 1980s, First Lady Nancy Reagan led the fight against drug addiction with her public plea to "Just Say No" to drugs. The point was clear and unwavering as a primary weapon in her fight against illegal narcotics, especially to youths.

She wanted to get current and future drug abusers to say the little word *no* to combat a growing epidemic of substance abuse. The catchphrase of her campaign was both straightforward and bold in its logic. The simple "just say no" message quickly spread through the culture in the days before social media.

In our widespread battle against the noise that's both inside and all around us, the same phrase can be applied as a solution. Say no more often and drown out the noise in your life.

The Power of Self-Mastery

Too simple?

Not really. There is power in self-mastery. As old-school as it might sound, we have the power within us to choose what to tune out and when to tune in.

So, even though the "Just Say No" campaign on drug abuse didn't succeed *broadly*, "Just say no to noise" can work for you on a *personal* level.

Repeat this simple declaration: I say no to noise.

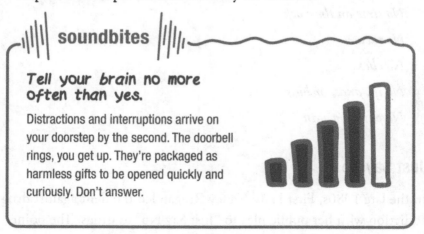

soundbites

Tell your brain no more often than yes.

Distractions and interruptions arrive on your doorstep by the second. The doorbell rings, you get up. They're packaged as harmless gifts to be opened quickly and curiously. Don't answer.

Overcoming FOMO

One of the biggest challenges we all face is the fear of missing out, commonly called "FOMO." We might feel something like this:

"I've got to check that text right now because it might be important."

"I need to scroll indefinitely through my social media feeds because I might miss something."

"I have to check another option because I haven't seen enough choices."

"I always have to be on e-mail because it's expected I reply immediately."

We all recognize that this behavior isn't healthy, productive, or viable, but we all continue do it. We are afraid of missing out. It makes sense. Who wants to miss something that's critical—an alert, a call, a breaking news story?

Yet, we all make a pact to search constantly through haystacks of useless information looking for the needle that might be there. It not only wastes valuable time but also trains our brains to respond immediately and impulsively to triggers with constant anxiety and senseless anticipation. FOMO is hard to resist.

No, Here's How You Do It

How do you say no when you face the daily expectation to keep up? What is the risk versus reward for parents, managers, teens, and professionals?

Author Greg McKeown says essentialists believe that making things better means eliminating something. It's true that in a great movie, many good parts have to be edited out. It's true in writing that editing must be a ruthless practice.

Overcoming FOMO is a serious challenge that requires some strong virtues:

1. **Fortitude.** An inner strength and courage to make frequent choices to miss out.

2. **Conviction.** A commitment to embrace fewer, not more, things.

3. **Trust.** An instinct that tells you what seems alluring and essential is probably just mindless noise.

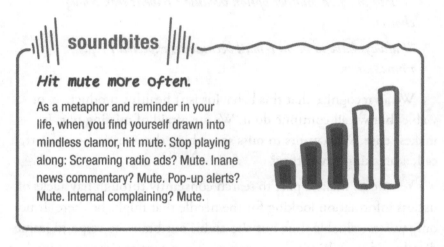

soundbites

Hit mute more often.

As a metaphor and reminder in your life, when you find yourself drawn into mindless clamor, hit mute. Stop playing along: Screaming radio ads? Mute. Inane news commentary? Mute. Pop-up alerts? Mute. Internal complaining? Mute.

Addictions Weaken Willpower

In a video about the addictive power of technology, Judson Brewer, one of the authors of *The Craving Mind*, describes how the brain is wired through a cycle of triggers to respond in order to achieve rewards.

He talks of feelings (e.g. fear, hunger, anxiety, isolation, etc.) that provoke impulses to achieve a promising resolution. For instance, he describes a moment of boredom that might prompt us to check our phone in hopes of finding something interesting and meaningful and, instead, encourages, "Just be curiously aware of what's happening in your body and mind in that moment. It will just be another chance to perpetuate one of our endless and exhaustive habit loops or step out of it. Instead of seeing a text message, compulsively texting back, feel a little bit better, notice the urge, get curious, feel the joy of letting go and repeat."[1]

This cycle, he cites, can create constant cravings—and instant rewards—over time, from which the brain makes powerful and permanent habits, ones that we might need to consciously try to break later on.

In essence, these triggered responses can become addictions that weaken our ability to resist.

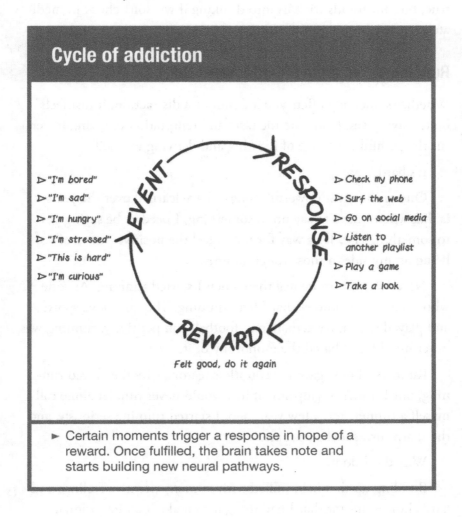

Cycle of addiction

▷ "I'm bored"
▷ "I'm sad"
▷ "I'm hungry"
▷ "I'm stressed"
▷ "This is hard"
▷ "I'm curious"

EVENT

RESPONSE

▷ Check my phone
▷ Surf the web
▷ Go on social media
▷ Listen to another playlist
▷ Play a game
▷ Take a look

REWARD

Felt good, do it again

▶ Certain moments trigger a response in hope of a reward. Once fulfilled, the brain takes note and starts building new neural pathways.

In our own circumstances, the habit of turning to noise (e.g. giving into distractions, permitting interruptions, and embracing multitasking) all undermine our ability to focus and train our minds toward craving this impulsiveness, often completely unaware it's even happening.

Before we can even think about saying no to an unexpected text alert, our minds desire another dopamine release that promises that the next message might mean we hit the big jackpot. It never comes true, but our minds trick us into thinking if we don't check immediately, we might not win the lottery.

Running to Yes on the Road Toward No

Whether somebody offers you a donut or a distraction, it just feels better saying yes. Compare the taste and temptation of giving in versus the painful challenge of resisting and denying yourself.

It's hard.

One of the most powerful things I have learned over the years is that when I have to say no to something, I need to be saying yes to something else. It's a way for me to feel the positive power of yes being on my side in those tough moments.

Never was this more real than when I started running. Anyone who's close to me knows that I hate running. Though I love sports and played soccer, basketball, and football competitively, running was never my thing. I hated the monotony of it.

Runners I know gave me countless reasons why they loved running, but I wasn't buying any of it. I would never run, let alone call myself a runner. Yet, a few years ago, I started running seriously, and the sharp turn shocked people.

Why did I do it?

Building up that habit, filled with so many negative feelings and hard choices, meant that I had to fight to make it an intentional

··{ NOTEWORTHY } ····························

Emotional noise rising

The root causes of what triggers the debilitating sounds between our ears

Emotional noise isn't just another type of noise but is the root cause of how we react to other types of external noise in our lives. Author and leadership coach John Erickson strongly contends that until we acknowledge it as the source—not a symptom—we will struggle with managing what's wasting our time and what's draining our energy.

"It's so subtle that we don't recognize it's happening until after it does," he says. "We respond out of what our internal noise is telling us to do rather than what our rational or thoughtful mind might do."

Erickson says that emotions are built into us. They aren't good or bad but simply part of who we are and can be important indicators, like you see on a car's dashboard when the oil or fuel is low. We don't get mad at the light but look at the problem it's indicating. We need to acknowledge what triggers our emotions by looking at how three key areas aren't being met.

"Massive amounts of expectations, needs, and perceptions drive our day," he says. "Whoa, I'm getting frustrated, angry, sad, bored, confused, or anxious, what's happening around me? Those three things are triggers that can create static like you hear between radio stations."

Emotional noise is like the volume of the static, and the more out of control we feel, the louder it becomes. Lowering the volume coincides with a better understanding of why these three different emotion catalysts haven't been addressed.

What's more, when the emotional noise suddenly rises, it demands a rapid response—like when you hear a loud noise.

"It's a fight or flight response when it goes from a low 1 or 2 to a 10," he says. "And if we decide to flee—or isolate—media consumption and Internet addiction are easy ways to medicate the pain and become a false reward that we believe will make the emotional noise go away."

Bottom line: This is noteworthy because emotional noise rises and rages inside all of us. We not only need to know why it's being triggered but also need to recognize how we can easily be deceived into using distractions, media, and digital devices as empty solutions to soothe us.

Dr. John Erickson is a leadership consultant, co-founder of Eden Business Concepts LLC, and author of *Three Paths Out of Paradise* and *Discovering Your Path Through Conflict* (www.edenbusinessconcepts.com).

priority. With a busy schedule, I needed to find ways to resist complacency and the constant temptations to blow it off, not to mention to overcome my deep disdain for it.

So how did I get the power to say no to my wide variety of reasons to avoid running?

I found a simple, powerful reason to say yes as an offset. For me, it was tracking miles on an app. It felt like I was collecting gold stars as a simple reward, and it worked to keep me running for almost two straight years. What drove me was finding a reason to say yes while also having to say no to my internal arguments and laziness.

When it comes to saying no to noise, we have to say yes to something else.

Find your counterbalance.

Self-Control Is a Personal Way to Stop the Noise

When I was a kid, my dad had a million sayings. One of my favorites was "Let your no be no." He taught me so many things; among them was a constant reminder of what truly makes us human is our ability to choose.

He would say that the two faculties of the soul are our intellect and our will: our faculties to reason and think along with our capacity to decide. That made so much sense to me, especially at a young age. As I got older, I started to see that emotions also occupy a third place in us as well.

Our willfulness plays a critical role in noise reduction.

There's so much noise around us that disturbs, distracts, and defeats us. But being human means we can choose. It may not feel good to say no, and we might think and feel things that pull us in a different direction, but we can make that powerful little word work for us.

A decisive no can lead to noise abatement.

Impulse Management: A Few Daily Distractions

During the course of a day, there are so many moments when our minds get yanked around, latching onto things that really don't matter much. It happens so frequently that you might not even notice how draining it can be.

Here are a few instances where you can practice impulse management:

- **Passerby.** You're sitting at your desk reading an important e-mail and somebody approaches. Your curiosity awakens. Who is it? Oh, it's so-and-so. Great, now you either have to say hi or pretend you didn't see them. Back to work. Say no.

- **Notifications.** Bing, bing, bing. You hear the phone alert go off while talking to a friend. Maybe a text or a weather update. Like Pavlov's dog, you instinctively pick up the phone and read the alert. You've lost your mind yet again—and maybe your friendship. Say no.

- **Ideas.** Walking across your house to get scissors, you start wondering if you have anything clean to wear tomorrow. You quickly cut to thinking of tomorrow's appointment and recall you haven't accepted the invitation yet. You grab your laptop and forget the scissors. Say no.

Feel the Peace of Singlemindedness

Set your mind to one thing at a time. Be convinced that this will build focus and bring peace. Use any one of the three previous examples and let yourself feel it: keep reading and finish the e-mail; hear the notification, but stay in the conversation; walk across the house and get the scissors.

Strength and Barbell Logic
Voluntary hardship meets modern weakness

Strength training seems like an appealing thing—for some people. I held this belief until I met my own strength trainer, Kathryn, and then discovered a peculiar podcast called *Barbell Logic*.

The podcast co-hosts, Scott Hamrick and Matt Reynolds, got me hooked from the onset.

"It's a philosophical and social crusade for me to help these old people and young people launch their lives and become adult human beings," says Matt.

Scott chimes in, saying, "In today's age, a self-confident, healthy, mentally tough human is no longer the norm, it's the exception. But strength produces the exception."

I loved listening to them defining strength as the ability to produce a force against a load, then string pearls of wisdom characterizing such strength as critical, essential for us to handle life's day-to-day burdens and difficulties.

Strength changes your confidence because you've conquered things that are hard, and you've conquered things that are heavier than what you might face today. You've embraced voluntary hardship to endure involuntary ones like losing a job, getting sick, being tempted by constant distractions, and incessant choices.

"When we talk about strength, we're not talking about an ethereal thing, we're not talking about mental toughness," they add. "We're actually talking about physical, moving-a-load strength, the ability to produce force against an external resistance. For us, that thing that provides that external resistance is the barbell, with weights. Stronger people are harder to kill."

Bottom line: These two are noteworthy because developing real physical strength paves the way to mental toughness, resiliency, and discipline, which is essential to living in a world of noise and not succumbing to its empty allure.

The podcast *Barbell Logic* is available at https://barbell-logic.com/.

Our minds want to focus on one thing at a time. Multitasking doesn't bring peace of mind; it breeds a divided mind. As we become more aware of our awareness, we can flex our willfulness muscle more to embrace less. And when we do, we should remember to feel that feeling.

It's a better way to be.

Five Small Steps to Make That Little Word a Big Part of Your Life

1. **Say it out loud.** Hearing yourself say no is very different than thinking it. Tell someone, "No, I can't talk to you right now" or "No, I am not interested." Or tell yourself, "No, I'm done with checking e-mail for the day" or "No, I am not going to do four things at once."

2. **Mute small distractions.** Search for some simple, maybe silly things to avoid. Maybe it's not changing a song to find a better one, putting your phone in the back seat while driving, or placing the TV remote control far away.

3. **Say yes to something else.** Any distraction, interruption, or invitation to shift focus needs to be met not only with a sharp "no," but also with a compelling "yes." What is your personal reward when you resist more noise?

4. **Embrace your "why"—no excuses.** Justifications, pretenses, and rationalizations to juggle more will get you nowhere. Decipher why succumbing to more noise will only debilitate you.

5. **Five out of seven isn't bad.** Don't be a perfectionist. Avoiding noise all the time is improbable and unlikely. Dialing it down more to even half of the time will make your life better.

Rewind

- Do you notice yourself interrupting conversations or your work when you are distracted by alerts on your phone?
- Do you feel guilty if you say no to something even if you know you already have too much to do?
- What is one area of your life where you can immediately begin to practice willfulness?

[Brief Recap]

Saying no is a powerful expression of our willpower. Many of us have a fear of missing out, or FOMO, that can cause us to produce useless static in our lives. We need to say yes to tuning in, when we are saying no to tune out the noise.

{Tune-in}

By getting used to saying no to little things in life, we can reduce or eliminate lots of daily noise around us.

14 Quiet Time: Restoring and Recharging Your Mind

S top right now and listen to what's around you. What do you hear? Music? An alert from your phone? A news anchor chattering on the TV or radio?

The nonstop noise that surrounds us doesn't abate. As the Kenny Chesney song "Noise" sadly observes, we had no role in getting it all started and little power to shut it down.

Clearly there's need for more quiet in our day. Time to think, rest, reflect, and recharge.

We have opportunities to do this, yet we don't take advantage of them enough. For example, on our commute we can turn off the radio for a few minutes. Sitting down after school or work, we can unplug from technology for a few minutes. At the end of the day, we can go to sleep on time, without one more look at our smartphones. In the moment, we can spend time in silence before the day begins.

Quiet is our weapon to counter noise.

Our brains crave quiet yet it's elusive, and we resist seeking it. Spiritual writers prescribe that we dedicate daily moments for prayerful reflection, and mindfulness experts share tips on meditation practices. There are even apps dedicated to relaxation and stress reduction. All of this is meant to calm and center our brains, but if you talk to anyone who has tried to follow any of these exercises seriously, they'll tell you how challenging it is, at least at first.

Dedicating some time for quiet is a hard but worthwhile habit. Our brains are high-performance engines that race at high speeds, so we need to let them cool down or they will start to smoke.

Hit mute more often

We need to be decisive and say no when useless information competes for our attention.

Dimly Lit Dinnertime: Our Brains Barraged and Batteries Drained

Imagine a couple like Matt and Marta on a typical weekday. They both have complicated schedules. There are bills to pay, e-mails to answer, conference calls to take, long commutes to endure. They run from activity to appointment, returning phone calls, scheduling carpools, and making plans. Setting aside time for each other is practically impossible.

Their kids aren't immune to their own noise. They are always connected to school, sports, side jobs, and social media.

Over the course of a typical weekday, the entire family exerts precious mental energy focusing on so many competing priorities and trying to keep up.

"It's hard to slow down and focus on being a family," says Marta. "Matt and I see how things have changed dramatically over the past 10 years and how draining it is for all of us."

When dinnertime comes around, everyone's brains are still buzzing, and their commitments aren't slowing down.

"We made a choice to make dinner a sacred moment where the chaos and connectivity are left at the door," Matt shares. "No phones, no interruptions, and no calls—just quiet time to be together."

Every day they battle the temptation to embrace hyperconnectivity and all the noise around them instead of setting aside time for personal and family connections. Yet, they make a concerted effort to hold fast and set rules for simple conversation that puts their priority on each other.

"We each talk about a high point and a low point in our day and what's happening tomorrow," Marta says. "It's made us a better family. We like being together, and it restores us."

Sadly, many families miss these quiet moments and dive back into the chaos of a constantly connected, busy world.

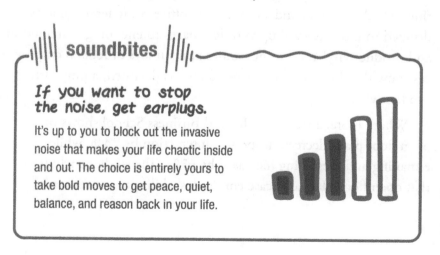

soundbites

If you want to stop the noise, get earplugs.

It's up to you to block out the invasive noise that makes your life chaotic inside and out. The choice is entirely yours to take bold moves to get peace, quiet, balance, and reason back in your life.

The Extrovert Ideal and the Allure of Open Spaces

Modern workspaces have opened up all around us. Gone are the days of offices with doors and privacy. The open concept design for homes has followed with great rooms connecting what used to be two or three different rooms into one common area.

So why the push for architectural openness? Blame it on extroverts.

Susan Cain, author of *Quiet: The Power of Introverts in a World That Can't Stop Talking*, told NPR: "It's quite a problem in the workplace today, because we have a workplace that is increasingly set up for maximum group interaction. More and more of our offices are set up as open-plan offices where there are no walls and there's very little privacy . . . The average amount of space per employee actually shrunk from 500 square feet in the 1970s to 200 square feet today."[1]

Our society places a value on being collaborative, creative, and in constant contact with each other. We now work in what amounts to large coffee shops where clamor and creativity sit on a pedestal, and privacy and focus are a footnote.

About two decades ago, the US General Services Administration, which manages and supports the offices of federal agencies, decided to move toward open office spaces to encourage interaction and productivity. Yet, recent studies and surveys of federal employees show that interaction between staff has declined, along with productivity.[2]

What's more, a study by Harvard Business School shows that open floor plans decrease in-person interaction by 73%, while e-mailing and messaging increased by 67%. The study concludes that open floor plans decrease employees' ability to concentrate.[3]

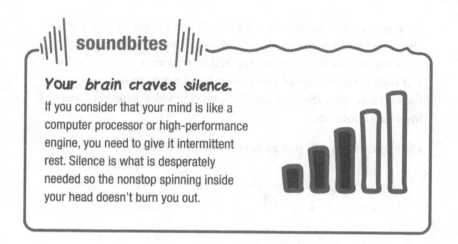

soundbites

Your brain craves silence.
If you consider that your mind is like a
computer processor or high-performance
engine, you need to give it intermittent
rest. Silence is what is desperately
needed so the nonstop spinning inside
your head doesn't burn you out.

Why Be Quiet? (I've Got Something to Say About That)

We all need attention liberation.

According to *Psychology Today,* approximately 50–75% of people are said to be extroverts.[4] It seems that our world is designed by
them and for them. An emphatic value is placed on what extroverts do naturally: make small talk, share opinions freely, and shine
socially.

Though I'm exaggerating a little, this might ring true if you're an
introvert.

So why is quiet time so important? It's not meant to hush extroverts but rather to get all of us to rest, think, and recharge. We need it
because we're all overstimulated.

Our attention needs to be freed, not fried.

According to Daniel Goleman, author of *Focus: The Hidden
Driver of Excellence*, quiet time is needed for the same reason we
need to recover after physical exercise. However, he warns that not all
activities are recuperative.

Such restoration occurs when we switch from effortful attention, where the mind needs to suppress distractions, to letting go and allowing our attention to be captured by whatever presents itself. But only certain kinds of bottom-up focus act to restore energy for focused attention. Surfing the Web, playing video games, or answering emails does not.[5]

Our brains require rest as much as our bodies.

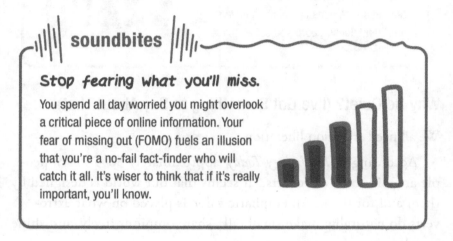

soundbites

Stop fearing what you'll miss.

You spend all day worried you might overlook a critical piece of online information. Your fear of missing out (FOMO) fuels an illusion that you're a no-fail fact-finder who will catch it all. It's wiser to think that if it's really important, you'll know.

Risky Isolation

Isolation can be healthy if it equates to a momentary separation from activity in order to reduce stimulation and regain energy. This is something introverts pursue naturally and extroverts may need to attempt more intentionally and forcefully. Even unplugging for 10 minutes can make you feel like you're being antisocial, yet the benefits are immediate and real.

The serious issue, however, is when isolation becomes permanent separation. As human beings, we need real connection with each other.

A study by the global health service company Cigna found that "nearly half of Americans report sometimes or always feeling alone

(46 percent) or left out (47 percent)" and that "Generation Z (adults ages 18–22) is the loneliest generation and claims to be in worse health than older generations."[6]

Extroverts can risk isolation when they use their down time to stay online, playing games that don't require other people. Introverts can further avoid human interaction and turn to quiet time as a way of cutting themselves off from the friendships and contacts so vital to them.

In either case, quiet time needs to be a realistic chance for us to recharge and regain our mental energy to focus on important matters that require our precious, depleted attention, not just to disconnect from others or avoid them altogether.

Rewarding Isolation

Quiet time's reward is that we give ourselves time to think and reflect. In their book *Lead Yourself First: Inspiring Leadership Through Solitude*, Raymond Kethledge and Michael Erwin make a compelling case for how effective leaders can take advantage of momentary isolation, stepping out of the hectic connectivity of their daily circumstances to seek clarity and direction.

In the introduction, they write,

Leadership, as Dwight Eisenhower defined it, "is the art of getting someone else to do something you want done because he wants to do it." That does not mean that leadership amounts to using people; like anyone else, a leader must recognize that each person is an end in himself. It means, instead, to make others embrace your goals as their own. But to do that you must first determine your goals. And you must do that with enough clarity and conviction to hold fast to your goals—even when, inevitably, there are great pressures to yield from them. To develop that clarity and conviction of purpose and the moral courage to sustain it through adversity requires something that one might not associate with leadership. That something is solitude.[7]

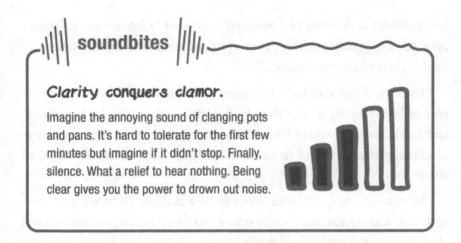

soundbites

Clarity conquers clamor.

Imagine the annoying sound of clanging pots
and pans. It's hard to tolerate for the first few
minutes but imagine if it didn't stop. Finally,
silence. What a relief to hear nothing. Being
clear gives you the power to drown out noise.

Steps Toward Quiet

Here are some suggestions for increasing quiet time and achieving
strategic solitude in our lives:

1. Go to Sleep!

If something is valuable, we need to schedule time for it. This starts
with sleep, which we don't get enough of in our busy, tech-tied lives.
The statistics are staggering:

- 35% of adults sleep less than seven hours a night.
- Only 16% of college students admit to getting eight hours of
  sleep a night.
- Teenagers need to sleep more than nine hours a night, yet most
  are lucky to get seven.
- 86% of students take their phones with them to bed.[8]

Personally, I've seen this become a serious issue with my kids
when they enter high school. By the time they're in college, the habits
worsen. Sleep patterns are all over the place and I can see the effects
clearly when they get enough versus not enough.

One of the many benefits of consistent sleep is that the brain can achieve what scientists call "consolidation," a magical way the brain strengthens memories and practices skills you learned. What's more, the health benefits of sleep are many, including reducing your risk for cancer, heart attacks, and strokes. It also reduces stress and can help people with depression.

2. Practice the "7-to-7" Rule

In a survey we conducted at The BRIEF Lab, nearly 70% of people admitted that checking their phones was the first and last thing they did every day, myself included.[9] To combat this debilitating tendency to become addicted to devices, I challenged myself to set daily limits.

After 7 p.m., I put my phone away and I don't check it until 7 a.m. the next day. It's hard. I battle the fear of missing out on something. I also battle the urge to check social media and to send a late-night e-mail. But this habit not only reduces my daily screen time, it sets boundaries to allow for other regenerative activities like reading, conversations, meditation, and exercise.

3. Look Forward to a Walk

Taking a simple walk does marvels for your mind.

Melina B. Jampolis, MD, author of *The Doctor on Demand Diet,* says, "Research shows that regular walking actually modifies your nervous system so much that you'll experience a decrease in anger and hostility."[10] It also exposes you to sunlight, which helps stave off Seasonal Affective Disorder.

You can set aside time for a short walk, whether it's first thing in the morning or later in the day, to clear your head and process what's happening in your life. It might be as simple as walking the dog or taking advantage of walking versus driving.

I encourage you to do this, but remember that it's easy to make excuses. I'm an expert at excuses. Yet every time I walk, I feel better.

I notice it especially helps me when I travel. I take advantage of every moment to recharge and refresh. Walking through an airport terminal or in a new city, I look straight ahead and walk. That way the walk doesn't lead me to curiously seek out more distractions. Rather, it's simply for my mental health to prepare for the day ahead or recharge from a long one.

4. Unplug for 11 Minutes

In the mock documentary about a rock-n-roll band, *This Is Spinal Tap*, Nigel Tufnel infamously tells reporter about his powerful amplifier:

Nigel: "If you can see, all of the numbers all go to 11. Right across the board. 11. 11. 11. 11."

Reporter: "Most amps go up to 10."

Nigel: "Exactly."

Reporter: "Does that mean it's louder? Is it any louder?

Nigel: "Well, it's one louder, isn't it? It's not 10. You see, most blokes are going to be playing at 10. You're at 10 here, all the way up, all the way up. You're on 10 with your guitar. Where can you go from there? Where?"

Reporter: "I don't know."

Nigel: "Nowhere. Exactly. What we do is if we need that extra push over the cliff, you know what we do?"

Reporter: "Put it up to 11?"

Nigel: "Eleven. Exactly." [11]

Rather than just taking a 10-minute break from your laptop or smartphone, consider going to 11.

Why?

As Nigel Tufnel said, "What we do is if we need that extra push over the cliff, you know what we do? Eleven."

You can prove to yourself that you need that little extra boost of silence. Think of it like the anti-amplifier. It's being even more intentional about the need for silence.

5. Find Your Own "Cabin"

If you're a busy person who's always on, you need to get away for a few minutes during the day. Think of it like magically escaping a busy city and instantly finding a quiet place in the mountains.

Since your home, office, and school are designed to promote disruptions and distractions all around you, how do you escape? You need some imagination and determination to find or create a space that limits noise and preserves quiet. It certainly won't be easy, but the payoff will be significant.

At work, you might find an empty office or unused conference room or make a "do not disturb" sign and buy a pair of noise-canceling headphones. At home, you might set aside a room or even a chair and table as a sacred space to read, think, and rest. At school, using the library, a study hall, or sitting in an empty classroom might do the trick.

Take a look at the spaces around you that can serve as a refuge from the deluge of your hectic days. Find them and use them.

····{ NOTEWORTHY } ·····························

Lowering noise levels
Headphone and earphone technologies that keep out the racket

One effective way to keep unwanted sounds out is to wear advanced headphones or earphones. There's a noticeable reduction in noise, nearly eliminating unwanted sounds around you, whether you're on an airplane, at the gun range, or in an office.

There are differing technologies to achieve this end, each taking a different approach. According to Stephen Kohler, former marketing leader at Shure, a leading global audio electronics manufacturer, there are separate ways to lower the noise and enhance the sound.

Sound Isolation

Shure Incorporated has been a pioneer in developing sound isolating earphones and headphones. Simply put, this technology virtually eliminates external noise through a design by which the earphone inserts into the ear in such a way that almost no external sound can enter, creating what they refer to as an "immersive experience." Shure's approach is so popular that many professional musicians use their earphones as part of Shure's Professional In-Ear Stereo Monitor Systems (PSM®) to help hear themselves on stage in a context of 120-decibel volume levels.

Noise Cancellation

Bose Corporation, another global leader in the audio industry, has been a pioneer in the development of noise-canceling technology. In this approach, an electronic process is used by which a microphone inside the headphone detects external noise and active circuitry creates a mirror image that creates a canceling effect to the listener.

Bottom line: These two technologies are noteworthy because they give us practical ways to protect ourselves from noise.

Stephen Kohler is founder and CEO of Audira Labs LLC, an executive coaching and leadership development firm dedicated to helping professionals grow by becoming better listeners. He's a musician and executive with over 25 years of global leadership experience, including with Shure Incorporated.

Contemplatives in the Middle of the World

There are dozens of small ways that we can insert quiet into our modern lives. It's not just taking a nap, going for a brisk walk, or finding a safe, silent haven at work.

Centuries ago, people who felt a strong religious calling would leave society entirely and form monastic communities. One of the more well-known saints to lead this movement in Christian tradition was Benedict of Nursia, who formed a monastery in Italy, in 529 AD, where men would leave the world and become contemplatives, dedicating their lives to prayer and work ("ora et labora"). There was very little said that wasn't directed to God. They spent eight hours a day in prayer, eight hours working, and eight hours sleeping.

In the modern tradition, my parents belonged to a religious organization whose founder proposed an intriguing version of the ancient monastic tradition that was uniquely designed for modern, busy lay people. Their vocation was to become "contemplatives in the middle of the world." He encouraged ordinary people to live daily practices like an hour of silent prayer, reciting the rosary, and meditating quietly on scripture. Many of these practices, it turns out, are ways to let your mind unwind and recharge.

Before getting married, my dad was briefly connected to the Alexian Brothers, a Catholic religious order. Although that vocation was not meant for him, he felt the strong appeal of the life of quiet, contemplative prayer.

He and my mom would have all of the kids join them in praying the rosary in the car driving from place to place. Looking back, it was something they wanted to do, and if we were with them, well, we were on board, too. It was generally boring, but it was something we did as a family.

If you're unfamiliar, the rosary is a repetitive prayer that cycles short devotions over and over again out loud ("Hail Mary, full of grace . . . ." "Glory be to the Father, and to the Son . . . .").

Now, more than ever, those practices have both a deep spiritual and mental value. They let the brain unwind and wander. They don't force the mind somewhere but gracefully permit it to drift toward contemplation and rest. Ironically, it let my young mind unwind and drift to sleep many times in those car rides. I needed it then, and my kids need it even more now!

Rewind

- Think about your average day. What are things that regularly steal your attention and distract you? Can you eliminate one or two to eliminate some noise in your life?

- Which of the previously mentioned steps can you incorporate into your daily routine? A walk? Better sleep? Unplugging for 11 minutes? Meditation?

- What spaces in your home, office, or school can you use as a daily "cabin"?

[Brief Recap]

All of us need time for quiet each day to relax and recharge our minds.

{Tune-in}

Make the intentional decision to do one thing each day that brings quiet into your routine.

15 Present Listening: A Gift Worth Giving Now

Few people know how to listen well, or even care to learn. It's tough on so many fronts. We're super busy, generally distracted, and more concerned about our own thoughts, perspectives, and plans. Who has the time and mental energy to listen actively and deeply to someone else?

It's draining to listen.

Yet, it gives you power to reveal hidden insights, deepen understanding, and build stronger connections. Think of the people you know who are gifted listeners. Do you know more than five of them? Probably not. What stands out when you're in a conversation with any one of them? How does it feel? What are their secrets?

The term *present listening* is my intentional play on words. It means both that you are in the moment—not racing ahead or looking back, but in the here and now—and giving your listening as a gift, not expecting anything in return, with little to no agenda.

Present listeners have a power to lower the noise and get themselves, and others, to tune in.

While developing our workshops at The BRIEF Lab, my initial focus was developing a curriculum on becoming a concise communicator. Over time, however, the value of listening as a core skill of any effective communicator emerged like a bubble to the surface. Truth be told, I had little to add because I wasn't a strong listener. Though I had my moments, active listening was not a strength at the time. My late brother, Johnny, who also taught classes with me, was an exceptional listener and insisted we teach this skill.

On his advice, I decided to design a practical homework exercise on active listening for our two-day course participants. The assignment was to engage in a 15-minute conversation with someone and just be aware of your awareness while listening. In other words, listen to what your Elusive 600 might be screaming in the middle of a conversation.

The shared results have been a mix of painful anecdotes (e.g. calling an ex-girlfriend and talking for three hours), surprising successes (e.g. breaking through to a tough teenager), and hilarious failures (e.g. sleeping on the couch). One story in particular stands out among the countless I've heard over the years.

A soldier in an elite military unit recounted his difficult listening assignment to me and his teammates the following morning.

"It was an epic failure," he stated bluntly. "My wife walked out on me."

He said, "I wanted to do an amazing job, so I started some 'assault listening,' not 'active listening,' with her. I wanted to do the best in the class on the exercise."

"She walked into the kitchen and started talking all about her day. I have never listened to her more closely in my life. It was amazing," he shared. "She was going on and on, but I stuck in there and was hanging on her every word. And then my mind started drifting to the kitchen counter. I saw something spilled on it."

"I kept listening but my mind pulled me toward some powder on the counter. I started wondering if it was lemonade or sugar or something. But I kept on resisting the urge to check it out because I was doing such a great job listening," he boasted.

"And then I decided I could break contact for a millisecond and clean up the powder," he said. "And as soon as I turned my head and lost eye contact, she screamed 'you never listen to me' and stormed out. My listening exercise was over because we have no kids and only two dogs."

"I wasn't about to stop, so I called Pizza Hut to find someone to listen to," he said to the class as we all sat stunned. "This kid answered and all I said was, 'How was your day, do you like your job, and what kind of delivery car do you drive?' The kid panicked and hung up on me."

Assault listening isn't active listening. Deciding to be good doesn't translate into success right away. Practice makes all the difference.

Why Is It So Exhausting to Listen?

Paying attention requires mental energy. In many instances, it's not obvious what people are trying to say or where they're going in a conversation. All the while, our Elusive 600 starts firing off comments, criticisms, and questions, or just starts heading into a different direction altogether.

It is hard to stay engaged, especially when we have bad habits and lots of handy excuses:

- My mind is racing all over the place.
- My environment is all wrong.
- Technology is momentarily more interesting.
- People are way too hard to follow.
- I've heard all of this before.
- It doesn't matter, and I really don't care.
- I've got something better to do.
- There's no end in sight; when is it going to stop?

Active listening means being engaged and involved, asking better, more directed questions. It's far from passive listening, which is difficult but not that hard. Good listening is a powerful way to lower the noise and heighten focus and concentration on both sides. It jump-starts good conversations.

Professional Listeners: It Pays to Be Interested, Not Interesting

There are a few professions where active listening is an essential skill. If you think about a firefighter, an accountant, or a graphic designer, listening isn't typically on top of their job descriptions. You'd like them to be daring, conscientious, and creative.

But there are a few professions where listening separates the good from the great.

Three professions come to mind in which people get paid to listen closely. In each, what's their primary aim? In every one, they're far more *interested* than *interesting* and listen with acute purpose.

- **A journalist listens to . . . reveal a story.** If you put a proven journalist in almost any environment, they will find a story. Conflict, characters, and resolution.

- **A therapist listens to . . . uncover pain.** When a patient sits in a psychologist's office, after a while they will share hidden traumas, inner conflicts, and personal burdens.

- **An interrogator listens to . . . unlock inconsistencies.** A witness or suspect will disclose tidbits of information that help piece together the puzzle of an unsolved crime.

In all of these jobs, the professional listener isn't just listening *to* someone but, more importantly, listening *for* something. The distinction is enormous because they listen with pointed purpose and deep interest.

► Present listening is an essential skill that sets you apart and lowers the noise.

Becoming a Present Listener—Seven Critical Considerations

There's not a single component that can make you an effective listener. With so much noise in your head and all around you, however, your ability to shift interest in the moment from yourself to someone else is possible, with effort and practice.

It's almost as if you magically acquire the combined superpowers of freezing time while becoming selfless. No small feat.

Here are the key characteristics:

1. **Be present.** Don't fast forward or rewind back but stay in the moment. It's all about right now, so be patient.

2. **Be interested.** Ask better questions. It's much better for you to be attentive, involved, and concerned about the speaker than to try to stand out, tell your story, or give your opinion.

3. **Know that it's not about you.** Give the gift of yourself and your attention, and you might get something surprising in return. Just don't expect it right away.

4. **Have little to no agenda.** Try to avoid forcing a predetermined direction or engineering a specific outcome. Expect the best in people, and let the conversation flow freely with good questions to guide it.

5. **Be understanding.** If you're looking to agree or disagree, you're missing the point. Listen to learn and comprehend, with concern and empathy.

6. **Be ready to suffer (a little).** Your willingness to be kind and patient will feel pleasing to people, although it might be somewhat painful to you. Remember, it won't kill you.

7. **Understand it's a decision, not a feeling.** There's a reason so few people are good listeners. It's a choice they make to focus on someone else first, not follow momentary emotions.

Each of these characteristics adds up to something much larger. The focus becomes someone else, not yourself. The shift is noticeable.

A Special Reward for Special Forces

Present listening is the key to unlocking some tough doors.

On one occasion, a student of mine, who is a Green Beret, shared how he was able to forge strong ties with someone at a high level within the State Department. While being deployed overseas, he had to interact with a variety of senior staff at an embassy.

"I'm an introvert and so was the ambassador," he shared. "We had to travel together and it was awkward because nobody liked talking much and there was a lot of time spent in the car. I started thinking about his job and all he had to do to get there, so I asked, 'How did you get into this line of work?' It was a harmless question and I was interested in hearing his answer."

That simple question started a conversation that spanned the half-day ride. A few days later, my student was standing in the hall of the embassy with his teammates, and the ambassador greeted him by name as he walked down the hall.

"How does he know who you are?" they asked. My student answered, "I just said, 'We had a really nice conversation a few days ago.'"

During the course of that conversation, and many others like it, I discovered a hidden bonus of learning more about people. It's not being nosy or manipulative but genuinely wanting to know people better. That's how friendships and deeper connections form.

Selling Yourself Short with Others

Sales people are notoriously bad listeners. They're too busy talking. The best ones are a breed apart and love listening and learning more than hearing the sound of their own voice.

I had the privilege to be a keynote speaker at a national sales conference. I spoke to more than a few thousand sales professionals about how to have better conversations; the role of listening took center stage. During my remarks, I shared the story of the ambassador and Green Beret's car ride. At the end of the story, I asked all of them how many of them knew how their clients started their career.

The room was silent.

If they knew present listening, their sales numbers would be off the charts.

The Payoff of Present Listening

People notice when you care.

My brother Johnny had this gift in spades. He was a really interesting guy and a great storyteller. But more than anything, he was deeply interested in others. Everyone fascinated him and quickly became the center of his attention: nieces and nephews, co-workers and classmates, and perfect strangers on a plane. His love for people was magnetic. The many people who knew him felt it.

Listening and focusing on others was among his greatest gifts.

People felt his care and concern—and remembered. When he was truly present, he was able to hear things that other people generally missed. He got to know people better, more personally.

You can capture comments, insights, and preferences, whereas other people give up or change the subject. People talk to you and feel safe opening up about themselves in surprising ways. You play a pivotal role in making their noise levels go down and help them tune out the chatter in their own lives. You have conversations that are memorable and that matter.

··{ NOTEWORTHY } ·······························

A noisy environment proves to be a breeding ground for a new book
Listening in a frantic moment produces critical guidance

Some settings are noisier than others. As a staff officer at Joint Special Operations Command (JSOC), Tom Earnhardt worked with elite professionals, tackling mission-critical deadlines, managing dozens of issues and people with urgent priorities who competed for attention and action.

"I quickly learned that noise was a way of life, so I trained myself to tune in to my boss and stay close to the pulse of the command," he said.

In 2010, Rebecca served as the Public Affairs Officer for one of their nearby units. She was new to the community, coming to grips with the noise in her own environment. Her leadership was wrestling with an expanding mission, constrained resources, and real concerns about their internal and external communication.

"I was very aware of her problems and the noise she was navigating," he commented. "But they were her problems, not mine. So, I let her figure it out —until she called me with an urgent request."

She was tasked to build a strategy to revolutionize the way their unit communicated in challenging environments to very diverse audiences. Rebecca shared the bold, nearly unrealistic, request and Tom acknowledged the challenges and agreed to help her. He admits she was almost paralyzed by the predicament, with little idea where to start.

"I was now sucked into her problem," he said. "So, I asked for time to think and said I would contact her in a few hours."

Tom admits that he became keenly aware of his own intense noise at that moment. Yet he listened to her and created quiet time to contemplate a thoughtful solution.

"Initially, I had no idea how to help her," he thought. "But I took time to reflect, 'who do I know that might be able to help?' Almost five years earlier, I had a similar monumental task, and I met a marketing agency executive who made a trip to Fort Bragg from Chicago to help my then boss, Major General Caldwell, to prepare to serve as the spokesman for Multi-National Forces in Iraq. So, I made the call and introduced him to Rebecca."

Bottom line: This story is noteworthy because Tom stopped to listen, giving himself quiet time to develop a solution. It's also worth mentioning that he called me that day, which started my journey to help fix that problem, write the book *BRIEF*, and now the book *NOISE*.

Few people have this gift, and even fewer give it.

As I mentioned earlier, you probably don't know five people who listen like this. Be one of those five people, and you'll stand out.

Rewind

- Do you pay attention and maintain focus in conversations or are you distracted by internal or external noise? Are you a present listener or are you merely pausing as you wait to interject your own point or opinions?
- Who comes to mind when you think of someone you know who is a good active listener?
- How can you become a present listener and extend that gift to yourself and others?

[Brief Recap]

Make a commitment to practice the habits of present listening to connect more deeply and to build stronger, more personal connections with family, friends, and colleagues.

{Tune-in}

Listen with purpose, giving the gift of your individual attention and time, to lower the noise around you.

Part Four

Getting Others to Dial In: Focus Management (FM 101)

16 Focus Management 101

Focus management is the responsibility of getting others around us to improve their attention. As they drown in information, we stand on solid ground and throw them a lifeline. Our clients, co-workers, and kids might get swept out to sea since they are so heavily addicted, connected, and distracted that they cannot resist accessing more information and giving into more diversions.

They need us to do something drastic and different to help them out.

I want you to see yourself as a "focus manager." This is an unofficial job title you can carry into a variety of circumstances and relationships. This hidden badge of honor might save people you know from going deaf by succumbing to the nonstop noise that is becoming their new normal.

As we have discussed earlier, improving your own attention is a personal responsibility, protecting your own brain from the bombardment. Though we maintain this responsibility, we have to be realists and recognize that our families, companies, and connections won't immediately embrace the challenge without us stepping up and helping them out. They may be unaware of the threats or consequences of infobesity or struggle to have the discipline they need to lock in on the most essential things in life.

You need to assist them when they can't help themselves.

It's time to unplug

Shhh! It's quiet time!!!

Changing an Environment That Doesn't Want to Be Changed

Noise begets even more noise.

Pervasive screens project static rather than insight, wisdom, and knowledge. Technology is at the heart of a heartless push for more noise consumption. It's not a pretty picture. Here are some staggering statistics from *Statistica* about what happens every minute:

- 4.3 million videos are watched on YouTube.
- 2.1 million snaps are shared on Snapchat.
- 13 million texts are sent.[1]

The world needs to stem the tide of the flood of information. Stopping the barrage won't be easy. Who's up for the challenge to become a focus manager?

Putting Fun Back into a Party

Several years ago, my daughter Joanna had a fifteenth birthday party. She was in high school and invited about a dozen girls over for the evening. Since it was late March in suburban Chicago, it still wasn't warm enough to be outside.

As her friends started to arrive, my eight-year-old daughter, Marta, did something unexpected and amazing. Joanna's friends all had smartphones and Marta knew they'd be using them all night long. She decided to grab a large plastic container and tell (not ask) all the girls nearly twice her age to put their phones in the bins as they entered.

As I stood nearby, I heard her say confidently and boldly, "Put your phones in here. They'll be safe, and you can get them at the end. You'll have a lot more fun."

I was stunned—and so proud. What a leader. Nobody told her to do it. She stepped up, knowing the difference in engagement would be enormous.

She was right.

Over the course of the evening, all the girls were involved in all the activities. None of them felt inclined or tempted to post on social media or check their phones. It was a bold move that ensured they'd have more fun.

And they did.

Years later, Marta had her own party and did the same thing. It was a little harder as she got older, but she realized her friends would have more fun.

Same results: more focus and more fun.

···{ NOTEWORTHY } ·······························

Daniel Goleman's FOCUS
Breakthrough book on paying attention

There's lots to be said about the precious commodity of our focus—way too much, ironically. In fact, there's so much being written on this topic that it's pretty easy to tune most of it out.

Not so for this classic.

In the words of Goleman, "Powerful focus brings a sense of peace, and with it, joy."

The chapter titles tell the story: Anatomy of Attention; Basics; Attention Top and Bottom; The Value of a Mind Adrift; Self-Awareness; Seeing Ourselves as Others See Us. The list goes on.

Not only is it engaging and well written, relevant, accessible, and applicable, I couldn't stop taking notes as I turned the pages.

In particular, one chapter really stood out to me, "A Recipe for Self-Control." Goleman emphasizes the need for impulse management and how it plays a critical role in all of our lives. In it, he relates how paying attention to self-control is a predictor of success:

"The big shock: statistical analysis found that a child's level of self-control is every bit as powerful a predictor for her adult financial success and health (and criminal record, for that matter) as are social class, wealth of family of origin, or IQ. Willpower emerged as a completely independent force in life success—in fact, for financial success, self-control in childhood proved a stronger predictor than either IQ or social class of the family of origin."

Reading this book was as refreshing as it was rewarding.

Bottom line: This book is noteworthy because it captures the inherent value of our attention, top to bottom, and serves as a timeless point of reference to all facets of this skill in our lives.

The Role of a Focus Manager

Nowadays, we need to play the same pivotal role as my daughter Marta. We need to help others who struggle to pay attention avoid the constant allure of noise that distracts and detracts them from really living.

We have to step up.

Here's a list of some of the attributes a person needs to lead others to improve their attention:

- **Leadership.** Takes charge when others accept the status quo.
- **Clear communication.** Speaks and writes clearly, simply, and concisely.
- **Single-mindedness.** Core concern is improving others and their environment.
- **Unapologetic.** Doesn't ask permission. On a mission.
- **Selflessness.** Cares deeply about the well-being of others.
- **Discipline.** Has willpower to say no consistently and decisively.
- **Courage.** Not afraid to be a contrarian.

Entire environments become inundated with useless noise, and people become used to hearing it. It's not just kids hanging out but also parents, professionals, and friends. Someone needs to take the initiative to ensure these settings don't become places of mindlessness packaged as business as usual.

The few need to start whispering "enough" to the many.

One person can change society. Though this has proven to be true throughout history—for good and bad—it may seem unrealistic for most of us to be that person. What can you do when the force and pressure of information overload is stacking up against all of us? Can you scream "stop" and expect things to change? Will complaining silently serve anyone?

It only takes one dedicated person to start a noise-abatement movement.

In such a noisy world, a great place to start influencing and shaping change is within your immediate environments: schools, homes, offices, and social circles. Start small in some of the following ways:

- **Meetings that don't matter.** Are you willing to demand a better agenda or walk out if a meeting is pointless?

- **Family time with faces down.** Are you asking people to talk to one another at mealtime and not be online?

- **Social media unfriended.** Are you willing to decrease social media sharing about a sandwich you ate that isn't worth anyone's time? Or unplug entirely?

- **Tech love lost.** Are you opting more for paper and pen versus screens and tablets?

- **Expecting always-on.** Are you practicing patience and not criticizing people who don't respond right away to your texts or e-mails?

However small they might seem, each of these moments carries weight. We can shift the paradigm and expect something different. Gone is the status quo, and it starts with small steps.

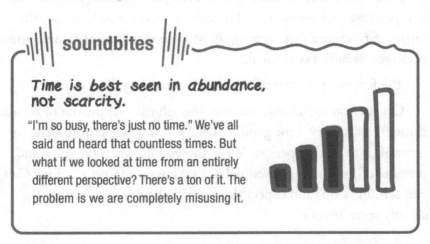

⁞⁞⁞ soundbites ⁞⁞⁞

Time is best seen in abundance, not scarcity.

"I'm so busy, there's just no time." We've all said and heard that countless times. But what if we looked at time from an entirely different perspective? There's a ton of it. The problem is we are completely misusing it.

A Program Manager for a Life Filled with Simplicity and Clarity

The job description of "focus manager" would read like this: "Leader wanted to help throngs of friends, families, and colleagues to stop worrying about useless information, echoing mindless sentiments, and contributing to information addiction. Must be strong, love silence, and crave clarity."

Yvonne was one such leader, at work and at home.

A single mother with three kids and a career professional, Yvonne was someone who wasn't afraid to go against the grain. Her kids were above average in school, active in sports, and had lots of friends. Yet, from a young age, they were used to her telling them no when other parents were much more lenient.

She was strong-willed and wanted to develop her kids into well-balanced adults, who practiced self-control, could focus on what mattered, and knew how to avoid the static and chatter of adolescence.

Professionally, Yvonne had little tolerance for meetings with all talk and no action. She set some rules about limiting time on e-mail after hours and on weekends. In conversations with clients, she always led with better questions and practiced more acute listening. They loved her attentiveness and asked to work with her by name.

Yvonne's desk was less cluttered than those of her colleagues, and her boss always got a straight answer from her, leading to more responsibilities and assignments.

Simply put, she was dialed in at work and tuned in at home. She wasn't going to let either environment change her.

So, she changed her environments.

FM Pre-set Buttons

When looking for a favorite station on the radio, we can program pre-set buttons for easy access and focus. Likewise, we can help others manage and set their focus more consistently and predictably.

Here are the practices that I will explain in the upcoming chapters that I suggest you learn to become a master of focus management:

1. Be better; be brief.
2. Communicate like a magician.
3. Prepare, organize, and design environments.
4. Lead like you're herding cats.

These pre-sets can help you become a qualified focus manager.

Rewind

- What was your first reaction to Marta taking away the girls' phones at the party? Do you feel stressed at the thought of not having your phone with you? Are you relieved by the thought of having it away from you only for a while?

- Can you pick an environment in your life where you can begin to practice focus? Maybe it's having your family and friends turn off their phones when you're sharing a meal. Start small.

- Which of Yvonne's habits can you adopt and incorporate into your own? Can you use these habits to begin your work as a focus manager?

[Brief Recap]

Our friends, family, and co-workers are inundated with and addicted to noise. They need "focus managers" like us to help them break free.

{Tune-in}

Begin to think of ways to make yourself a focus manager.

17 Wanted: BRIEF Communicators

B lah, blah, blah.

We've all grown accustomed to hearing lots of noise. Another meeting (blah, blah, blah). Getting a safety briefing (blah, blah, blah). Checking for more e-mails (blah, blah, delete).

As the words pile on, it's hard not to ignore most of it.

What if we could be consistently clear and concise? The value of receiving communication that's brief is golden. An infamous writer, known for his brevity, once shared his secret by saying that he intentionally would leave out words people would probably skip.

Be brilliant, be brief, and be gone. Imagine what our world might look like.

- What if the meeting started with a clearly stated objective and agenda? It would save precious time and improve productivity.

- What if the airline safety briefing clearly stated the risks? It would ensure passengers were ready to respond in an unexpected emergency.

- What if the subject line of an e-mail provided a point up front? We'd confidently open it, quickly grasp the message, and know how to reply.

Frustration is a term I've heard defined simply as an unfulfilled expectation. When it comes to our communication, people around us anticipate brevity but get irritated and annoyed when they have to sift through long, complicated messages. They constantly struggle to find the main points as they drown in useless and inessential information.

They expect brevity as a lifeline and drown when it isn't thrown to them.

When So Many Words Become Worthless

We hear jargon so frequently we don't even realize how our brains treat it as static.

Strategically leverage platforms to scale growth. Turnkey solutions to optimize enterprise impact. Initiate cross-selling opportunities to improve share of wallet.

It sure sounds important—but it's worthless.

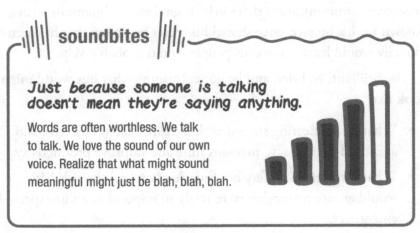

soundbites

Just because someone is talking doesn't mean they're saying anything.

Words are often worthless. We talk to talk. We love the sound of our own voice. Realize that what might sound meaningful might just be blah, blah, blah.

Does it help people understand what they need to know? Working with professionals and executives, I see buzzwords pile up all the time. When people use "corporate-speak," they're trying to project knowledge and authority. It's also a kind of shorthand suggesting, "I'm an insider." They don't even realize how they're training others to ignore them.

Yet too often, these words don't give listeners what they crave: a clear message with real meaning. Instead, they're dished out like verbal junk food—empty calories with no nutrition.

The *Wall Street Journal* made light of this when they launched their Business Buzzwords Generator. Basically, the generator randomizes words. It's scary how much some of these suggested phrases sound like real stuff we hear from people every day:

"We need to vertically taper *our* optics.*"*

"We need to strategically empower *our* wheelhouse.*"*

"We need to literally silo *our* value add.*"*

"We need to horizontally unpack *our* incubator.*"*[1]

I dare you to drop one of these in your next meeting. I bet no one would even notice. Maybe that's part of why we like jargon. Because we can say stuff with relative certainty that no one will take issue. But the real risk is that our audience will just ignore us and move on. We're training them to tune us out.

Losing the Meaning

I was in Phoenix, Arizona, for a national sales meeting where The BRIEF Lab ran a boot camp for a company that was undergoing some big changes. When we asked the salespeople to put their company's story into their own words, something interesting happened: they kept reverting back to standard buzzwords to express their ideas.

Throughout the workshop, we challenged them to tell us an authentic story about where they've been, where they are now, and where they're headed next as a company. We wanted them to briefly and genuinely answer a simple question from their customers, "Hey, what's new with the business?"

Once they adjusted, their stories got real and started to stick.

With attention spans on the decline and information consumption on the rise, we need to communicate concisely to be absolutely sure people will hear and understand us. Buzzwords may seem to telegraph competence, but it just leads to more confusion.

Speaking and writing in clear and simple terms is rare.

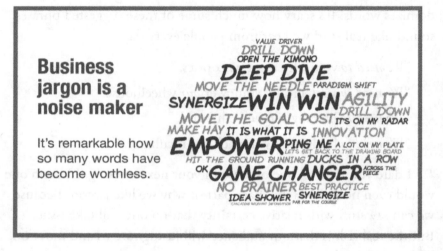

Business jargon is a noise maker

It's remarkable how so many words have become worthless.

You Can Change It

What can we do to stop ourselves and others from becoming human generators of "custom-built meaningless business phrases" like that *Wall Street Journal* randomizer? I recommend two things:

1. **Be more aware:** Jargon has become a bad habit. Notice your word choices. Make an effort to be more conscious of the words you use. Encourage others to do the same. You'll be amazed at how often you and the people around you reach for these junk-food phrases. Eliminate them.

2. **Keep it simple:** This is a trick that we teach in our courses: when you notice yourself saying something needlessly complex,

just add "in other words" and rephrase it using more ordinary words. What comes out is much simpler and clearer—it's what you were actually trying to say.

"Corporate behavioral attitudes and values" might become "the way we work around here." "Employee empowerment" could become "give people authority to make decisions."

When words lose their value, we end up with volumes of communication running through organizations that fail to move anything. There's lots of noise but little traction. Nobody wants that.

Message Lost in Translation

There's a risk when we communicate in such chaotic, info-laden tech traps. Our message can easily get drowned out. Parents with teens, teachers with students, managers with teams, and doctors with patients create more noise if they don't practice brevity.

What are people actually hearing?

A few years back, Indiana University's Tom Crean led the men's basketball team to a Big 10 season title. A camera crew caught his euphoria in the locker room afterwards. His pride for his players was powerful and contagious because they were not expected to win the championship that year.

As the players were celebrating, Coach Crean huddled them together to give them some final words to congratulate them.

"Guys, you've earned this memory," he said to get them to appreciate their huge accomplishment. Then he proceeded to talk for more than two minutes about a variety of things to make them value it even more. About a minute later, you could see his players start to lose interest; some of them even started clapping to signal him to wrap up his speech.

It didn't work. He kept talking, and his strong opening words got watered down in a meandering stream of comments and insights, most of which the players didn't even hear.

Why did he lose them in his passionate speech? He failed to keep it brief. A few words was all he needed to get the party started; it felt more like a class, or another pep talk.

Winston Churchill's Brevity Memorandum

In 1940, Britain's Prime Minister Winston Churchill was knee-deep in leading the defense of his country against a German attack. One could only imagine the number of daily meetings, discussions, and conversations he had to formulate the right battle plans.

At one point, he reached a boiling point and issued a one-page memo to his war cabinet with a one-word title: Brevity.

"To do our work, we all have to read a mass of papers. Nearly all of them are far too long. This wastes time, while energy has to be spent in looking for the essential points," he wrote, challenging them to keep their reports shorter and clearer. He concluded by saying, "The saving in time will be great, while the discipline of setting out the real points concisely will prove an aid to clearer thinking."[2]

Years later, Churchill's memo remains a challenge for most of us. Our role as a focus manager is critical: help people save time and zero in on what's most essential.

Concise Communication: A Necessary Curriculum Requirement

When I embarked on the journey to write my first book, *BRIEF: Make a bigger impact by saying less,* I was surprised at people's immediate response to its message. People started telling me how much they needed to learn this valuable skill, especially given how interrupted, inattentive, and impatient everyone is becoming.

My conversations revealed an education gap in the area of lean communication. If everyone is so buried and busy, how can they learn the basic skills of grabbing and holding others' attentions? As our focus erodes, the need to know how to master this skill set is crucial.

These skills and strategies need to be a direct and purposeful part of the curriculum at all levels of education and in the workplace. Whether one is writing an essay or an e-mail, talking with others in an informal or formal discussion, or participating in a college admissions or work interview, training and practice in implementing these skills may be the tipping point. Think of the positive outcomes: a higher grade, a successful sale, a promotion, a positive networking experience, or admittance into a top college.

I received an e-mail from a retired military member, Tamar, who was going to law school. She wrote to thank us for teaching her these BRIEF skills. "When I wrote my first paper for my legal writing course, I was very concerned because it did not match the elevated prose of my fellow students," she shared. "Well, I got feedback from the professor that my brevity and simple language was quite refreshing. He also added that the latest trend in lawyering is to write simply, especially in contracts, so the average user doesn't struggle to understand."

Like Tamar, increasing your "toolbox" of purposeful and concise language will positively affect those around you and make their lives better. That's what it means to be a focus manager.

I started The BRIEF Lab to help create an elite standard in concise communication. For both military and business leaders, our workshops, webinars, and keynote speeches not only help motivate them to embrace brevity but also arm them with practical tools to develop and deliver a message that is shorter and more impactful.

My vision has been to have the BRIEF methodology become an adaptive strategy and a gold standard that people can embrace to achieve greater results. They discover how to play a pivotal role in helping others around them consistently focus better.

Whether it's business people trying to sell a product, teachers struggling to keep students engaged, lawyers penning contracts, or friends having good conversations with each other, they all have something they need to do differently. By cutting, reorganizing, and delivering more concise information, they create better, stronger connections.

BRIEF Basics

To be an effective BRIEF communicator and an effective focus manager, you need to recognize a few common tendencies that distract and detract others from understanding what you're communicating.

Here are a few suggestions:

1. **Headlining:**
   a. **What it is:** leading with your most important idea first.
   b. **What it avoids:** the tendency to bury the point or miss it entirely.
   c. **What it does:** gets people's attention right away.

2. **Trimming:**
   a. **What it is:** removing burdensome information that weighs people down.
   b. **What it avoids:** making people struggle to weed through layers of detail.
   c. **What it does:** simplifies a message and lightens people's load.

3. **Mind mapping:**
   a. **What it is:** creating a visual outline that organizes your ideas logically.

b. **What it avoids:** having your communication seem dis-
jointed and rambling.

c. **What it does:** creates a smooth, logical flow.

Simplifying is one of the most valuable skills you can possess in a
complex world like ours. The BRIEF approach is a powerful way to
organize and structure information to make it much easier to consume. When trying to inform, explain, update, and convince, simplicity goes a long way.

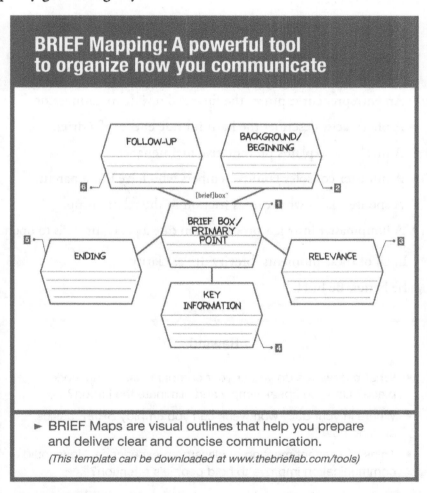

BRIEF Mapping: A powerful tool to organize how you communicate

► BRIEF Maps are visual outlines that help you prepare
and deliver clear and concise communication.

(This template can be downloaded at www.thebrieflab.com/tools)

Clarity Is Your Number 1 Priority

As Churchill's memo concluded, clarity is the payoff. When you receive static all day, you stop and notice when you suddenly hear a clear signal. Imagine going down the radio dial and finding a song that resonates. It stands out.

Focus management is handling people's inattention (their Elusive 600) and helping them zero in on what matters most.

The rarity is clarity.

In each of these situations, imagine how valuable BRIEF is:

- A parent justifies the importance of an unwanted punishment to their child.
- An entrepreneur captures the financial upside to an investor.
- A pharmacist describes the harmful side effects of a drug.
- A mechanic explains preventative maintenance.
- A minister consoles family members who have lost a parent.
- A spouse shares what causes friction in the relationship.
- A jumpmaster instructs procedures in case a parachute fails to open.

In all of these moments, brevity drives clarity.

Be better. Be brief.

Rewind

- What buzzwords do you or your company use in the workplace? Can you speak simply and eliminate the jargon?
- Where in your daily workweek can you employ BRIEF basics, starting now?
- Think of a recent meeting or classroom experience. How could communication improve to hold people's attention?

[Brief Recap]

We all are guilty of creating useless noise at work, school, or home. We owe it to others to cut down the fluff and to be brief.

{Tune-in}

Remove unnecessary and unclear noise from your communication, and people will hear you.

18 Communicate Like a Magician

Magic confounds us, entertains us, and, amazingly, gets us to focus on the *wrong thing*. When I think about you taking on the role of a focus manager, your responsibility is similar to the role of a magician, yet different.

You must get people to focus on the *right thing*.

As I was contemplating the successful communication techniques I've acquired and taught over the years that get—and hold—people's attention, magic came to mind: the art of conceiving a trick, planning, rehearsing, adjusting, and refining for days, weeks, and even months to get it just right.

There's something magical about a magician.

I once stumbled upon an episode of *This American Life* (Podcast 619, "The Magic Show"), and this insight came to life—effective communicators are akin to magicians. As I listened to host Ira Glass reflect on his fond memories of learning techniques as a childhood magician, I was mesmerized by the parallels to focused communication.

My mind raced to understand the connections.

"When you bought a trick, they took you to this special table in the back room and sat you down. And taught it to you one on one," Glass recalled. "As I remember it, this was done with kindness, with helpful tips—how to tilt your hand, how to turn your body, when to pause for effect. It was exciting being taken seriously by these men. Sharing those secrets."[1]

Whether it's hiding a coin, reading cards, or making the Statue of Liberty disappear, magic is the mastery of focus management.

In the same spirit, let's take a closer look at how magic and communication are kindred spirits. What are the secrets that effective communicators can employ to become masterful focus managers?

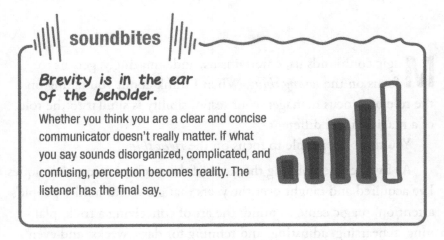

soundbites

Brevity is in the ear of the beholder.

Whether you think you are a clear and concise communicator doesn't really matter. If what you say sounds disorganized, complicated, and confusing, perception becomes reality. The listener has the final say.

Brain Science Behind Sleight of Hand

There's been significant research and analysis done by psychologists and neurologists about how magicians manipulate perceptions. Susana Martinez-Conde, author (along with Stephen Macknik) of the best-seller *Sleights of Mind*, said, "Magicians are these artists of awareness and cognition. These are expert manipulators of attentional levels."[2]

What she and other experts have uncovered is how effective magic tricks alter when and where you pay attention. The magician's techniques are powered by knowing exactly how our brains operate moment to moment.

For instance, when a magician moves their hand in an arc, the brain follows the movement from beginning to end. Were the magician to make a straight-line movement, the brain would anticipate that the hand is going from point A to point B, would then jump to B and snap back to A. It is important to have the audience's eyes moving continuously over the arc so as not to see something else that's happening in the trick.

This diversion of attention fakes out the audience, tricking the brain to see and focus elsewhere. What's more, the magician uses our hearing and innate love of narratives to manage large portions of our Elusive 600. While the magician is telling us a story, trigger words get our internal voices to start talking to each other, much like two security guards who just heard an unexpected sound. While they take time to investigate, the thieves break in.

It's all done intentionally, not accidentally.

The knowledge of our built-in assumptions and natural brain tendencies is at the core of magic. It's all planned, perfected, and proven to work not only on engaged and amazed audiences but also by neuroscientists.

The Power to Make the Restless Rest

In the Ira Glass podcast, he reminisces about being young and learning the tricks of the trade. He recalls feeling embarrassed because he was using store-bought tricks and beginners-level sleight of hand while performing in a tuxedo.

"And what I remember of the act, some of it was pretty corny," he said. "But at the same time, I can say for sure, audiences were engaged. They were engaged from beginning to end. People were not restless."[3]

His practice made perfect.

When you first adopt small communication techniques to get people to focus, you also might feel the same way: this seems contrived, silly, or even manipulative. It takes power to calm a distracted and divided mind. Like a magician, you will know and practice the techniques so well that people around you will connect magically to you.

Abracadabra

Magicians are masterful focus managers.

A Baker's Dozen of Communication Techniques, Tips, and Tricks

As the magician Raymond Teller of the famed Penn and Teller team once said, "If you understand a good magic trick—and I mean really understand it, right down to the mechanics at the core of its psychology—the magic trick gets better, not worse."[4]

Here are my "secrets" revealed to grab people's focus:

1. **"Name Calling"**
   a. **Principle:** Draws in someone personally and increases attention.
   b. **Picture it:** You're in a course with many students on the first day of school and the new teacher calls people out randomly by name. (*How does she know their names? What if she calls me?*)

    c. **Practice it:** In a conversation, mention the person by name twice, once near the beginning and another time toward the end. Don't do it too close together. Notice how their eyes move and how they tune in when you do it.

2. **"Good cop, bad cop"**

    a. **Principle:** Shows two extremes.

    b. **Picture it:** You get an e-mail message with the subject line "bad news and some good news." (*I need to open that one.*)

    c. **Practice it:** You're talking to a teenager, friend, or co-worker and ask them how their day was. Instead of asking the standard question, you say, "What was the best and worst part of your day?" See how frequently they stop, reflect, and answer more thoughtfully.

3. **"Flagging"**

    a. **Principle:** Promises an organized and measurable quantity.

    b. **Picture it:** You hear a joke that starts with "Three guys go into a bar and each asks for a pint of Guinness . . ." (*How is that one going to end? I've got to hear it.*)

    c. **Practice it:** In an e-mail, identify the number of points you want to make and state it first in the subject line (e.g. four ways we could improve safety) and then include a short sentence and four bullet points, ending with a simple call to action. Notice how quickly you get a response.

4. **"Story time"**

    a. **Principle:** Appeals to our love of narratives.

    b. **Picture it:** The new boss in a company calls her first staff meeting and opens with a short story about her biggest career mistake and how she recovered from the blunder.

(*I like her a lot already. She's a real person and learns from her mistakes.*)

c. **Practice it:** In an interview, answer a question with a short story that you've prepared in advance (e.g. when asked "tell me a little bit about yourself," say, "I'm resilient or goal-oriented. Let me tell you a quick story about why I'm like that."). Watch how they listen to you and how your story sets up their next question.

5. **"Picture time"**

a. **Principle:** Entices people visually.

b. **Picture it:** Parents want their kids to stay off their phones at the dinner table so they find a funny meme of a group of mindless teens staring blankly at their phones with a funny caption. They hang a copy on the refrigerator. (*I don't want to end up like a zombie smartphone teen addict, so I better follow their advice.*)

c. **Practice it:** In a presentation, use one large image per slide with a simple title above it. Since a picture is worth a thousand words, you will notice how locked in the audience is and how much more you control their distractedness.

6. **"The intermission"**

a. **Principle:** Gives everyone needed time to rest.

b. **Picture it:** You're right in the middle of an important planning meeting and the organizer unexpectedly calls a 10-minute timeout to break up the monotony. (*I like this person because they recognize how difficult and tedious the discussion has been. I love breaks and really needed one.*)

c. **Practice it:** In a heated, intense argument, ask for a few minutes for minds to clear and temperatures to come back down. Notice how when you resume, the intensity has diminished and the key issues come back into focus.

7. **"A hard turn"**

   a. **Principle:** Produces sudden, unexpected redirection.

   b. **Picture it:** Two people are conversing and one of them is monopolizing the conversation. The conversation is clearly headed nowhere. Realizing that she's lost her voice entirely, the focus manager interjects quickly, saying, "changing the subject completely ..." and steers the conversation elsewhere. (*I was going to be stuck in that conversation forever and really needed to grab the wheel before we drove off the cliff.*)

   c. **Practice it:** In a meeting that you see has gone far off course, step in and assert yourself, saying, "I think we need to jump back to the real reason we are here and restate the objective of the meeting." Watch how the rabbit-hole exploration suddenly ends, and you're all seeing daylight again.

8. **"Mindful and mixed metaphors"**

   a. **Principle:** Entertains the brain with hidden connections.

   b. **Picture it:** A mother is advising her daughter how to be more assertive as a young captain on a school sports team by telling her, "Honey, in some situations you need to grab the bull by the horns and run with it." (*My mom says the oddest things sometimes. Where am I going to find a bull to run with on the soccer team?*)

   c. **Practice it:** When you must explain something that is inherently complicated, try to find something to compare it to using *like* or *as*. (Examples: my job is like pulling teeth; being a project manager is like being a den mother with misbehaving teens; writing is as frustrating as golf; etc.)

9. **"Headlining"**

   a. **Principle:** Provides the bottom line upfront (BLUF).

   b. **Picture it:** You get home from work and ask your spouse, "How was your day?" Instead of saying, "Fine," their response is immediate and clear, "Our car now has a split personality!" (*Now I want to know what happened to the car and why it is acting so weird all of a sudden.*)

   c. **Practice it:** The next time you have to run a meeting, write down the point of the meeting in a headline that's no longer than eight words. Craft each word carefully and see how it directs and clarifies the conversation.

10. **"Amazing alliterations"**

   a. **Principle:** Produces predictably pleasant sounds.

   b. **Picture it:** You ask a close friend what his new girlfriend is like and he quips, "She loves to laugh and learn." (*I never thought he'd like to date a funny nerd.*)

   c. **Practice it:** When choosing words for a social media post, see if you can scan your vocabulary and select sounds that all start with the same letter. See how super simple?!

11. **"Q.C.O." (Questions, Comments, Observations)**

   a. **Principle:** Invites people to participate in the conversation.

   b. **Picture it:** You're watching someone make a presentation, and it seems like a typical monologue until she says, "I'm not going to do all the talking. Please take a minute to write down any questions, comments, or observations you might have." (*I'm so happy she took time to do that because I wanted to tell her how much I appreciated the stories she told.*)

   c. **Practice it:** At the end of your next presentation, invite the attendees to take a moment in silence to write down any questions, comments, or observations. (Note: Don't ask them to do it on the spot. Give them some time to think about it first.) Watch how this technique gets people engaged and talking.

12. **"The clapper"**

    a. **Principle:** Making real sounds creates real reactions.

    b. **Picture it:** A group of friends gets together for a surprise birthday party, and the host needs to get them to focus on what they all need to do in the final few minutes to create the surprise. He pops balloons unexpectedly, and they all quiet down. (*I was enjoying talking, but that noise really made me stop and pay attention to what to do before the lights dim.*)

    c. **Practice it:** The next time you're talking to someone and see that you're quickly losing their attention, try to make a distinctive sound (e.g. clap, snap, whistle, clang, pound, whisper, etc.) to alert them and draw them back in.

13. **"Memory recall"**

    a. **Principle:** Shows people you listened and remembered.

    b. **Picture it:** A salesperson calls a customer to check in with her a month after she made her purchase. During the conversation, he says to her, "Lisa, the last time we talked you said that your brother David's wife had a baby girl. So, what's it like to be an aunt? (*I love being an aunt, and I love that he remembered that detail. He cares about me personally and doesn't treat me like a typical client.*)

    c. **Practice it:** Jot down important notes and details that people share with you and reference them later, accurately and naturally. See how they appreciate that you could recollect a detail that most people would overlook.

All of these techniques and tips are simple, yet powerful ways to help people around you improve their focus. If done infrequently, none of them on their own will work that well. Like a magician, they take time and practice to master. But once you do, watch how mesmerizing you become as a master in focus management.

Rewind

- If you haven't seen a magic trick in a while, pull up a video of a magician on YouTube. Watch their gestures and where they attempt to draw your attention.
- Pick two of the "secrets" listed earlier and practice using them over the next week.

[Brief Recap]

Magicians are masters at drawing people's attention where they want it. We can use communication tricks of the trade to become masters of Focus Management.

{Tune-in}

Where can you use these "secrets" to help others pay closer attention?

19 Preparing the Environment for Noise Abatement

Noise is pervasive, entering not just into our offices, but also into our homes, cars, classrooms, and heads. Protecting ourselves from the constant barrage of mindless messages and streaming nonsense demands bold responses, starting with the basic environments where we live, learn, and work.

We need to design against distractions.

It's not going to be easy to set boundaries that limit and block unwanted access to noise. But we need to ensure our surroundings fulfill the need for more focus, rest, and real connections.

- When you walk into the average office or home, how many screens do you see?

- When you walk from conference room to cubicle, where does connectivity stop?

- When you go into a classroom without a connected device, can you still learn?

Who will redesign these spaces?

It seems like the architectural and design world is going with the flow, pushing an always-on agenda, from smart cars to smart classrooms to smart homes. Who will push back?

The Center for Humane Technology is stepping up, sounding an alarm with a conscience and with conviction:

> In the future, we will look back at today as a turning point towards humane design: when we moved away from technology that extracts attention and erodes society, towards technology that protects our minds and replenishes society.[1]

The Failure of Open Floor Plans

If you've ever worked in a building with few to no offices, at first it seems so inviting, creative, and collaborative. Yet, the day-to-day reality is that these environments breed distraction. It's like they were designed by extroverts to make everyone have to talk and force them to collaborate; yet it ends up being a constant fight to stay focused.

For a few years, my company leased office space in Chicago's West Loop, a trendy area with tons of office spaces in spacious lofts. Everything was wide open, and the few glassed-in offices we had looked like fish bowls.

My office had glass on two sides, and I felt as if I was always on display. Though it looked really cool, it was not conducive to quiet and more focused work. We were so collaborative that we interrupted each other constantly. And there was nowhere to hide or concentrate. It was wide open.

Research supports growing complaints from professionals who say that these environments look great on paper but are a painful and unproductive space in which to work. Certainly, you can cram more people into smaller spaces and sell it as a way to foster more

···{ NOTEWORTHY } ·····························

Learning a lesson in library school redesign
Creativity, collaboration, and communication bring in coffee talk—and some quiet

The modern high school is getting a makeover. Specifically, the look and feel of the library has shifted more toward a cool coffee shop and less like a haven for old-school silence.

According to Mark Skarr, Learning Commons Director in Naperville Community Unit School District 203 in Naperville, Illinois, getting the design changes right has been a real learning experience.

"We went from a traditional library to a learning commons environment. We needed spaces for students to be able to use technology and, more importantly, to have creativity, collaboration, and communication," he said. "There was a good TED Talk on coffee shops and how they were historically the place where great ideas came together."

His school dove in head-first. They started redesigning spaces and making them central locations to convene students and teachers organically to work together in different ways. The new design allowed many different seating configurations and was much more inviting. Glassed-in huddle rooms were added for focused work and deeper discussion, and a similar classroom provided for larger group collaboration.

"You now hear productive noise," he said. "We'll have nine different tasks going on, and the hum is an indicator of the kind of success going on."

He admits the design changes fixed one need yet exposed new ones: avoiding distractions and the need for quiet space emerged as concerns. Skarr acknowledged they needed to go further and add room for silence.

There are now dedicated environments for quiet, too.

"There's something to be said for big, open spaces, and small, silent spaces too," he adds. "The quiet spaces came because people started asking, 'Is there a room that we can do some focused work?' We had productive feedback giving them that valuable environment, too."

The encouraging sign is that both design spaces are available and always in demand.

Bottom line: This is noteworthy because going to open floor spaces creates opportunity for collaboration—and distractions. So, giving people a choice between silent and collaborative spaces is wise.

collaboration, but does it lead to more interruptions and distractions and to less privacy? In addition, in many of these open environments, there's practically no place to go for a private call or conversation, not to mention an area to work that's quieter and conducive to concentration.

In one study of these open environments, there was an ironic, noticeable increase in workers interacting less face-to-face and relying more on technology like e-mail and instant messaging to communicate. More research is showing that the spaces directly impact concentration. In fact, the main sources of workplace dissatisfaction were increased noise and a marked loss of privacy.[2]

The Institute of Psychology at the University of London suggests, "Your IQ falls 10 points when you're fielding constant e-mails, text messages, and calls. This is the same loss you'd expect if you had missed an entire night's sleep."[3]

The answer is finding balance and giving people options. Both collaboration and concentration need to be an equal factor in better office design schemes.

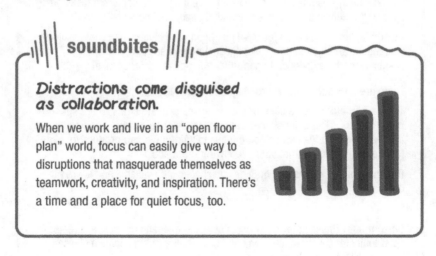

soundbites

Distractions come disguised as collaboration.

When we work and live in an "open floor plan" world, focus can easily give way to disruptions that masquerade themselves as teamwork, creativity, and inspiration. There's a time and a place for quiet focus, too.

Screens Everywhere at Work

It seems that office environments have embraced the vision to make technology and information ubiquitous. Walking into any corporate office is like wading through a sea of screens. It's not just conference rooms and lobbies, but kitchens, training rooms, hallways, offices, break rooms, and elevators. And with the relative cost of flat screens declining over the years, screens are becoming pervasive and invasive.

According to a research study examining society and culture in the workplace, author Ben Renner claims the average professional spends more than six hours a day in front of a screen.[4] In addition, experts predict that people will soon have access to more than six connected devices per person. The current average number of connected devices per person today is 3.64.[5]

What's more, mobile devices and laptops add to the mix.

In one client setting, I recall seeing people walking from meeting to meeting, all carrying their laptops from room to room. When they would sit down to start a workshop with me, they'd all open up their laptops and start typing. I'd be naïve to assume they were taking notes and not finishing up previous work or still on their e-mail.

So, what can we do to lead a redesign of our office environments? What are some smart, bold moves to put balance back into the workplace?

Here are a few ideas:

- **Ban laptops at meetings.** Make it a common practice to place laptops outside meeting rooms on a cart (with chargers and stacks of notepads and pens) to promote improved conversations and efficient exchanges.

Screens everywhere

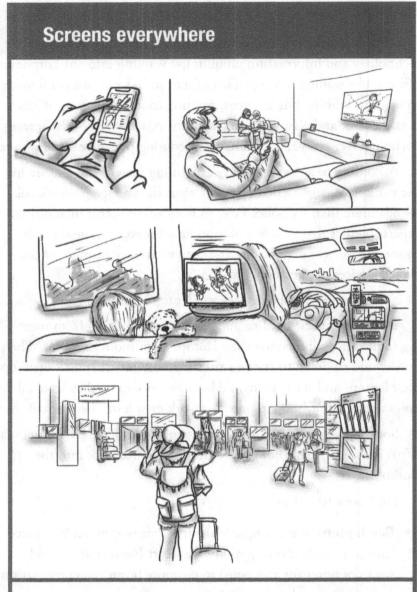

► Flatscreens, touchscreens, small screens, and big ones
  are popping up in every corner of our life, pumping
  information our way—whether we need it or not.

- **Check your phones at the door.** In secure military installations, there are lock boxes in which to check smartphones before entering the building. Install small cabinets with chargers and locks for phones and devices outside conference rooms and offices to promote fewer distractions.

- **Provide dedicated quiet rooms.** Like airport lounges and libraries, set aside spaces where silence is mandatory. This will provide people a designated place to go that fosters reflection, contemplation, and concentration.

- **Replace screens with whiteboards.** Ripping out a screen and repainting a part of a wall with Idea Paint fosters collaboration, conversation, and creativity.

- **Create Wi-Fi "cold spots."** In a visionary design, a Harvard graduate student proposed building small enclosures that prevented any connectivity to ensure quiet concentration. Consider expanding that design to select zones in an office.

So much of the noise we deal with professionally every day can be abated if we take small steps to reinvent and protect the spaces where we work. It starts with a thoughtful focus manager taking charge.

Home Rooms Unplugged

The environment at home seems a mirror image of today's workplaces.

When I was younger, television was going through an explosive expansion. It was pre-VCR days, and most households had, at most, two sets, most prominently in the living room.

In our home, we had our TV hidden in a wooden cabinet with a nice slide-out cover. To watch it, you had to open it by sliding the cover up and back into the furniture. Not only was it an ingenious design, but also a way to make the kids less tempted to watch it. It needed to be opened with parental permission, not just mindlessly turned on.

Looking back, what's noteworthy is that my parents not only wanted to keep our living room looking nice (having a big black TV tube in the center was hardly a design statement) but they also set some basic boundaries. Of course, TVs in the bedroom (and everywhere else) wasn't a thing yet. How times have changed!

In our homes, we need some select rooms to be off limits to technology, especially screens. The places where we sleep, converse, and most commonly connect at home should be off limits—even where we study.

We need to set some basic, protective design boundaries.

According to Joshua Becker at becomingminimalist.com, "Rooms serve purposes: kitchens are for cooking, dining rooms are for eating, and offices are for working. The better we define those rooms and their purposes, the more productive they become."[6]

Here are a few ideas that might inspire some functional, fundamental changes at home:

- **Artwork replaces monitors.** If you have monitors in many places, consider replacing one with framed artwork or pictures. Looking at family photos or a beautiful landscape is more calming and less distracting.

- **A room for reading.** If space allows, place a comfortable chair and some nice bookshelves in a space designated for quiet contemplation and reading. Having a dedicated nook at home is inviting and a reminder that rest and reading are close companions.

- **Storage for devices.** If you're like most people, you have phones, tablets, laptops, and plenty of charging cables all around. Find a dedicated box, shelf, or cabinet that not only serves as a hiding spot for technology but also provides a station to charge the items overnight.

- **Single-purpose spaces:** Whenever possible, designate a room for one reason (e.g. kitchen is for cooking, so no screens on the refrigerator; bedrooms are for sleeping, so no televisions, laptops, or phones).

Old-School Schools

In Silicon Valley, the Waldorf School has a distinctive vision of the educational environment. The school spurns technology almost entirely. In fact, about three-quarters of the students there are children of parents who work for technology companies. There are no tablets, screens, or smartphones, just face-to-face time and traditional education.

Ironically, their parents are the same professionals who develop applications, devices, and technology. They recognize the addictive qualities of these things and want to protect their kids from constant technology.

The rest of society is pushing for schools to embrace technology everywhere, from the classroom to the lunchroom. Although information technology is making many positive contributions, such as increased personalization, enhanced access to up-to-date sources, and improved parent-student-teacher collaboration, there are serious downsides as students ditch pencil, paper, and chalkboards for more smartboards and laptops.

What are some of the drawbacks of tech in the classroom?

- Distractions in the classroom
- Student isolation

- Teacher-student disconnect
- Reliance on technology over learning and critical thinking

Being a lone voice to stem the tide can be tough, especially when embracing technology amounts to modernization and keeping pace. What happens when teachers go contrary and want their students doing more hands-on science experiments, collaborative projects, and writing assignments offline?

How do we balance this reliance on technology with the potential dangers to students' socioemotional health and some core beliefs about the benefits of face-to-face interactions? How can we help students who are the first generation to spend their entire adolescence in the age of the smartphone balance their use of technology?

Here are a few ideas that might inspire some functional, fundamental changes at school:

- **Restructure the environment.** Move the laptops to a cart or keep the digital devices out of sight as lessons are taught and don't allow student access until the technology is needed as a tool for learning, not for the entire lesson or as a time-filler.

- **Provide both collaborative and quiet study spaces.** Create spaces in the classroom and in the school that can be used for small group meetings as well as quiet, reflective time. When designing lessons, teachers should plan for and practice "wait time" and "reflection time" so students can practice imagining, thinking, and problem-solving, either on their own or with a partner, so they aren't immediately going online for answers.

- **Promote activities and structures that don't rely on technology.** Design projects that begin with face-to-face conversations and interactions. Encourage discussion of group roles and purposefully model how to facilitate discussions instead of expecting students to innately know how to interact.

Remaking Healthy Environments to Filter Noise Naturally

Some of these changes are already being done as organizations thoughtfully design and promote living, learning, and working environments.

Human beings seek out environments with innate qualities like safety, security, and comfort. According to the University of Minnesota, healthcare facilities have made great strides to identify what aspects of our surroundings contribute to improved patient care and medical outcomes.

In their assessment, there are five primary considerations in planning these environments:

1. Providing an increased connection to nature with gardens or outside views.

2. Offering options within hospital rooms, such as adjusting their lighting, music, or temperature.

3. Enhancing social support with comfortable lounges and rooms to accommodate visitors.

4. Reducing environmental stressors by eliminating hospital noise and interruptions.

5. Providing pleasant diversions like artwork, aquariums, and fireplaces.[7]

This re-envisioning of the modern hospital could be the impetus to encourage others to change their environments for better care and better outcomes.

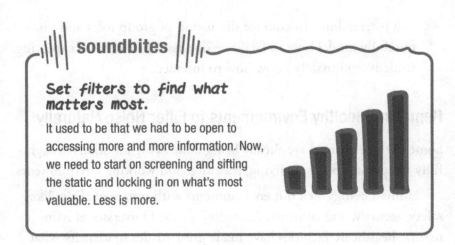

soundbites

Set filters to find what matters most.

It used to be that we had to be open to accessing more and more information. Now, we need to start on screening and sifting the static and locking in on what's most valuable. Less is more.

As we take on a leading role to help others around us focus more on what matters, whether that's at work, at home, at school, or on the go, we need to remember that all of these environments are in dire need of a makeover to become more peaceful and humane places for all of us.

Rewind

- Think of your home, office, or classroom. What features or technology promote an excessive, always-connected environment?
- What step or steps can you take today to put balance back into your workplace? How about at home?
- When you disconnect from technology, how do you feel?

[Brief Recap]

So much of the noise we deal with professionally and personally every day could be abated if we took small steps to reinvent and protect the spaces in which we work and reside.

{Tune-in}

Start building boundaries that limit and block unwanted access to noise in your world.

20 Herding Cats: Facilitating to Focus More, Fidget Less

Many years ago, there was a funny television commercial for EDS, a tech company that compared information technology consulting to herding cats. In the commercial, real-life cowboys shared the painful "realities" of being a cat herder.

"Herding cats. Don't let anyone tell you it's easy," one says. Another adds, "Anybody can herd cattle, but holding together ten thousand half-wild short-hairs, well that's another thing altogether." "Being a cat herder is probably the toughest thing I've ever done," yet another cowboy confesses.

What made that commercial so hilarious and instantly memorable was how it struck a chord with people. It got us to readily admit how humans can act as crazy as cats and how someone needs to round us all up.

Facilitation is one of the most important responsibilities of focus management. An elusive skill, it seems effortless when done well. Yet, the reality is that it's tough work getting people to collaborate, focus, discover, and discuss.

It's not easy making it look easy.

There are many distinctive domains where leaders can step up into the role of facilitator and focus manager. Three, in particular, come to mind: at work, at school, and at home. You may need to take on one or all of these roles at some stage in your life, each of them presenting separate challenges to get people to pay attention and stay on track.

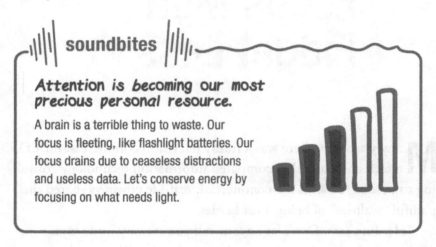

soundbites

Attention is becoming our most precious personal resource.

A brain is a terrible thing to waste. Our focus is fleeting, like flashlight batteries. Our focus drains due to ceaseless distractions and useless data. Let's conserve energy by focusing on what needs light.

The Joy of a Canceled Meeting

Meetings are typically tough. Whether they're too long, disorganized, or filled with tension and debate, most people would avoid going to a meeting if given the choice. Consider for a moment what emotion you would feel when you heard that a meeting on your calendar was suddenly canceled. The immediate response might be joy or relief.

Why?

Because few meetings are run well, with a stated purpose and a defined agenda. They're often painful and unproductive.

On average, business professionals spend 23 hours a week in meetings. Here's a quick snapshot of how meaningless they've become:

- One-third of all meeting time is considered ineffective.
- 92% of people admit to multitasking in meetings.
- Senior managers spend half their day in meetings.
- Executives consider more than 67% of meetings a failure.
- More than $37 billion per year is spent on unproductive meetings.[1]

Clearly, there is room for dramatic improvement. We must run better meetings, ones that people look forward to attending.

Teaching Students to Tune Out

The number of distractions that students face today is daunting. With access to connected devices, students have a constant choice between listening to instruction, looking at their laptops, or sneaking a peek at their cell phones when new texts arrive.

There are countless lures to lose focus, ranging not only from technology but also from lack of preparation, talking, and the environment itself. Beyond those temptations, many instructors are simply not engaging or are ill prepared to design lessons with a clear purpose.

► 92% of professionals admit to multitasking in meetings. 1/3 are considered ineffective.

Jorge, an assistant principal at a large, suburban high school, was in charge of evaluating teachers. He was specifically focused on the school improvement goal of incorporating technology into instructional design. Since the district had purchased laptops for all its students, teachers were expected to utilize them in the classroom.

Jorge first observed Brian, an experienced teacher, as he gave a detailed lecture on the Founding Fathers. Brian then asked students to research five facts regarding the writing of the US Constitution. He gave them 30 minutes to research and told them they would share their facts with the class afterwards.

Most students ran a quick search of "five facts about the writing of the Constitution" and then spent their remaining 25 minutes searching who was playing in the NCAA Sweet Sixteen, viewing the latest prom dress styles, or playing video games.

Jorge was appalled at the lack of planning, direction, collaboration, or interaction in this exercise. Yes, Brian used technology in his lesson, but students were simply regurgitating information and not engaged in meaningful work.

The next day, Jorge observed Elena, who had students read aloud a short poem by Langston Hughes, and did a quick round robin, asking questions to assess the students' knowledge of the Civil Rights movement. After consolidating and reviewing their answers, Elena defined a clear purpose for their use of technology, asking small groups to research assigned Civil Rights topics together, to find six cited pieces of information, and to create a slideshow with limited words and primary source pictures for their entire group to utilize in their brief presentation to the class.

Jorge noted students were engaged and purposeful in their research. Both teachers "used" technology in their lessons, but Elena was a focused manager with a defined agenda who helped students understand technology is not the lesson but is a tool to assist in the lesson.

The classroom is prime real estate for better facilitation.

Need Some Help Leading at Home?

Parenting seems to be getting even harder and the list of responsibilities longer. Of course, it always requires love, affection, and attention. Day-to-day, you have work, shopping, doctor visits, carpools, birthday parties, schoolwork, sports, budgeting, cleaning, and countless other concerns.

Now, add to that list running family meetings.

That may sound odd at first, but getting any family together, whether it's sitting down at meals, planning weekly activities together, or discussing the day's events, is akin to being a meeting facilitator.

Marcio, a friend of mine, shared a story of how he and his family coordinated selling their house and moving overseas.

> In the day-to-day chaos, we couldn't really talk about it at home as there were too many distractions. It became pretty clear that we didn't have a coordinated plan. My wife and kids weren't at all on the same page with all the things we needed to do over the coming months to get the house ready for sale and ship our things to France. I decided to take them to the local library and have a meeting. I had an agenda, and we had an open discussion to plan the move. It was a success.

Those same planning and facilitation skills come into play when arranging tech-free dinner conversations. There are too many competing priorities and choices that pull families in too many different directions and into more isolation.

Parents who want a better, more unified family life need to be facilitators to bring each other together.

{ NOTEWORTHY }

Dynamic meeting facilitation
Giving meeting attendees a "bill of rights"

For Tierah "Bob" Chorba, running a successful meeting is not only a big part of her profession, but also a passion. When I first met this expert facilitator, I was mesmerized by how she could calmly and confidently keep people focused and on task.

She made it look easy, and I knew how hard that was to do.

Her voice wasn't booming; she wasn't aggressive or pushy, just laser-focused on making the conversation easier for everyone. It was as if she had earned a PhD in meeting dynamics, deeply grasping what makes many of them go sideways with only a few of them successful.

"Great meetings happen by design, yet they seem like a rarity or an accident," she cautions. "One of the issues I combat is people wasting time and energy by not stating what they aim to achieve, the point of the meeting, in clear terms. The agenda is almost always vague."

Much to my surprise, she boldly challenges meeting attendees to push back more. She suggests that they need to exercise a bill of rights before a meeting even starts. That might include a few critical requirements: a clear, attainable objective; the reason their attendance is needed; a balanced discussion; realistic allotted time; and a printed agenda handed out in advance.

"We all know that meetings are generally a waste of time and unproductive," she states. "So, let's get people to challenge the status quo and demand from meeting organizers that their rights as productive professionals be protected, not abused."

Bottom line: Her approach is noteworthy because meetings are the source of so much painful noise, and we need to push back on the daily pain they cause in our professional lives.

Fundamentals of Facilitation: At Work, School, or Home

There are commonalties to being a better facilitator in the different environments of our lives. The key is finding ways to make it easier for people to focus. Your role is to make what's naturally difficult look simple.

Here are a few suggestions that I've learned over the years in each of these roles:

1. **Stay positive.** Setting the tone from the start is key. It's infectious when people see that you're encouraging, optimistic, and hopeful.

2. **Set some objectives.** Take time to prepare beforehand, whether it's picking a topic of conversation or defining a few goals. Say them out loud from the outset to set the stage.

3. **Prepare the environment.** Where you work, learn, or live together matters. Removing distractions, clearing clutter, and organizing the space translates into more cohesiveness.

4. **Get everyone involved.** Whether it's 3 people or 30, they all need to participate. It creates imbalance when some people are really active, while others stay passive.

5. **Ask better questions.** Getting people to talk, especially introverts, requires forming better questions far in advance. Building lists of open-ended prompts is essential.

6. **Manage the clock.** Know how much time you have and use it wisely. People's attention span will naturally deplete and everyone likes finishing up a little early.

Making It Easy for Everyone to Work, Learn, and Live Together

Developing the skills of facilitation requires time and effort and, most importantly, empathy. We feel the burden people carry being held hostage in bad meetings, we sense how easily students can sit mindlessly and learn little to nothing, and we care deeply that our families become more united and less isolated.

It's more than just helping people focus—life is tough, and we want to make it a little easier for others.

Rewind

- Think about the last three meetings you were in. Was there an agenda? If so, was it clear and adhered to?

- If you're a student, think of your recent classes. Is there an instructor whose lessons are easy to follow? What makes them clear? Is there an instructor whose lessons are difficult to follow? What makes them unclear?

- Think of a recent family dinner or event; how did everyone spend their time? Were they interacting or doing their own thing? What could have been done differently?

- Which suggestions for facilitation do you feel you could easily incorporate into your plans at work, school, or home?

[Brief Recap]

There are too many competing priorities and choices that pull workers, students, and families in different directions and into more isolation.

{Tune-in}

Developing the skills of facilitation requires time and effort but is crucial in order to help people in our environments focus and accomplish more.

Part Five

Pre-sets: Simple Programming for Noise Reduction

21 Personalizing Your Pre-sets

J ust as you program your radio to tune into your favorite stations or have preprogrammed playlists, you should also have some go-to habits that get you to dial into what matters most and tune out what's basically useless. These will help you to avoid searching aimlessly for more static.

Each of these pre-sets is meant to improve your AM (awareness management) and/or FM (focus management) skills. Consider trying a few from time to time to improve your noise abatement abilities.

- **Pre-set 1: Say no on the go**
  - ◆ **Premise:** Nobody plans to get distracted, interrupted, or derailed. It happens as unexpectedly as life takes its twists and turns. We need to be ready at a moment's notice to stay on course.
  - ◆ **Practice:** While you are commuting, pick one thought and stick to it. Whether you're driving or waiting to board an airplane or in line at the grocery store, avoid anything that might catch your eye or entice your attention, including checking your phone. That might mean not looking at that accident on the side of the road that causes a gaper's delay, not looking at a text alert, or not falling prey to the candy and magazine offerings that are strategically placed at the checkout line. Stick to one thought.

- ◆ **Promise:** Builds up your ability to say no to unexpected distractions and stay single-minded.
- • **Pre-set 2: Have a headline**
  - ◆ **Premise:** When you communicate in a meeting, a speech, or an important conversation, it is easy to lose people's interest in the first few seconds. We need to grab their attention boldly and avoid the slow buildup.
  - ◆ **Practice:** When you know you have something important to share, take a few moments to write out a short headline in advance. Keep it to eight words or less and make sure that it creates interest and points to what you're going to say. For example, if you know someone is going to ask you about your weekend, be ready to handle the obvious questions with a brief headline (e.g. Question: "How was your weekend?" Answer: "I need three days to recover," or "I think it was pretty weak," etc.). If people around you don't do this (e.g. in a meeting, e-mail, or update), challenge them to come up with a quick headline—it will only take a minute or two and will help grab and maintain their attention.
  - ◆ **Promise:** Sets the stage for people to listen when they might tune others out.
- • **Pre-set 3: Clutter clearinghouse**
  - ◆ **Premise:** Fear of missing out (FOMO) is a hard habit to break. We need to take drastic measures to avoid impulsively grasping for every tidbit of useless information.
  - ◆ **Practice:** Look around and find something that you own that you don't need or don't use that much. Maybe it's a pair of shoes, a pen, headphones, or a candle. It doesn't matter what the item is, only that it's something that you barely need, or might forget you even own. Go and grab it right now and get rid of it; throw it away or give it away. Don't hesitate. Just do it.

- ♦ **Promise:** Gets you comfortable with letting go. It helps you realize the power of being unattached from things—or information—with little or no significance.

- **Pre-set 4: MYOB (mind your own business)**

  - ♦ **Premise:** Curiosity killed the cat. So much of our wasted attention gets spent on thinking about things that are none of our business and never will be.

  - ♦ **Practice:** The next time you're with a group of people, notice how quickly your mind starts to formulate opinions, comments, and conclusions. Maybe it's about how they dress, speak, or organize their day; or where they live, what they believe, or where they went to school. Consider if any of these thoughts directly influence the way you live your own life. If it's an idle opinion, drop it.

  - ♦ **Promise:** Lets us reframe and tighten our focus on what really matters to us, letting go of futile thoughts and opinions.

- **Pre-set 5: Sound off on meetings**

  - ♦ **Premise:** Everyone complains about how meetings are a colossal waste of time and predictably unproductive. Yet nobody steps up and makes meetings more effective.

  - ♦ **Practice:** Take time to prepare and share a formal meeting agenda that outlines what's meant to be discussed and decided. Define the core meeting objective—the reason you're having it (and the risks if you don't). What's more, tell people how to prepare, who should attend, and why they're needed. Give them specific agenda items and allotted times for each. Finally, when the agenda is shared in advance, stick to your plan.

  - ♦ **Promise:** Gets you to retake control and establish new standards on how people can work together efficiently and effectively.

- **Pre-set 6: Take time with a timer**
  - ◆ **Premise:** Games end when the clock stops. When it's running, you play hard and play to win. The countdown motivates you to keep your head in the game.
  - ◆ **Practice:** Get a simple egg timer or a basic stopwatch. Don't use your phone, but something modest that makes an annoying noise when it runs out of time. Fix the time to 15 minutes at first and set a basic goal to tackle one thing, like writing a thank-you letter, cleaning a room, checking e-mail, making a call, or just sitting in silence. Like taking a test, stop the exact moment the buzzer goes off, not a second later.
  - ◆ **Promise:** Puts time limits on your side so you can start mindfully managing more moments throughout your day with greater awareness and intensity.
- **Pre-set 7: The 7-to-7 rule**
  - ◆ **Premise:** We are constantly checking our phones or electronic devices throughout the day—and night! Established boundaries can ensure that technology isn't the first and last thing you think about every day.
  - ◆ **Practice:** Consider where you sleep, whether it's at home or traveling. Place all technology a far enough distance away (preferably in another room), so that you can't reach it while lying in bed. You need to walk to get it. If you need an alarm, buy a cheap, small one. If you need to hear the phone ring, set it just loud enough to hear it from the distance. When you wake up, don't look at your phone until 7:00 a.m. and don't check it after 7:00 p.m.
  - ◆ **Promise:** Sets daily limits that protect you from technology becoming a bedside burden and lets you rest.
- **Pre-set 8: Talk a walk on the mild side**
  - ◆ **Premise:** Getting some simple exercise is a way to recharge your brain and disconnect from daily distractions.

- **Practice:** A few times a week, maybe even daily, go for a short walk. Don't treat this as exercise but consider it an opportunity to discharge all the static that's built up throughout the preceding day or week. Don't bring music and don't check your phone. Just walk and think of nothing, letting your mind wander. While you're walking, listen more than think, and look straight ahead, trying not to accomplish anything in particular.

- **Promise:** Provides critical moments to clear your head and restore focus.

- **Pre-set 9: Head down, heart up**

  - **Premise:** It can be hard to pay attention sometimes. In these moments, we need something to motivate us to dig deeper.

  - **Practice:** As you are tackling a particularly tough task like studying, writing, or listening, lean in a little more and consider why you're dedicating your undivided attention to the task. Sure, you're saying no to many other things you could be doing in that moment (like taking a break, checking an alert, or just zoning out). More importantly, consider what you're saying yes to and how it's worthwhile to make that momentary sacrifice to focus for a greater good.

  - **Promise:** Provides specific, meaningful purpose to your focus, especially in times when it gets really tough to pay attention.

- **Pre-set 10: Bag your bag**

  - **Premise:** You carry around bags of all sizes, yet rarely do you need most of what's inside. It's easy to get attached to stuff.

  - **Practice:** Forget your backpack, handbag, satchel, or briefcase just once. Go to school or work without it. If you start to panic thinking what might happen without it, take some time to empty it out and look at all the contents closely. What do you absolutely need that day? Only take that.

- ♦ **Promise:** Encourages you to realize how you are attached to things that you really don't need.
- **Pre-set 11: Tech timeouts**
  - ♦ **Premise:** Electronic devices and screens surround us, constantly competing for our attention. We need scheduled separation.
  - ♦ **Practice:** Whether it's during a meeting, a meal, a sporting event, or driving somewhere, give yourself, your family, and your colleagues a break. Don't use technology at all—even for music or podcasts. This isn't for the rare occasions like exotic vacations or being at a wedding, but as a regular, daily practice. Set a specific amount of time to disconnect, informing those around you. Hold to it completely.
  - ♦ **Promise:** Allows you to see how often you interact with technology, instinctively and impulsively. Feel how liberating—and hard—it is to take a break.
- **Pre-set 12: Feel some little feelings**
  - ♦ **Premise:** Without realizing it, we can miss small, yet important parts of our day. This can go on for a lifetime.
  - ♦ **Practice:** Look for three or four simple things you do unconsciously every day. Maybe it's taking a warm shower, drinking a glass of water, or sitting in a comfortable chair. While you're doing these things, feel what it feels like. Mindfully take notice. Sense the streaming warm water on your shoulders for 30 seconds. Taste the sips of cool water as you drink. Feel the coziness of the couch as you sit down in the morning or at the day's end. And truly experience it.
  - ♦ **Promise:** Gets us started tuning into and appreciating small moments of our day that can turn into something much more meaningful and rewarding.

- **Pre-set 13: Board games**
  - ◆ **Premise:** There's nothing like an old-school game such as Monopoly, Jenga, or Solitaire to help you unwind. Games play an important role in letting our brains recover from the barrage of noise.
  - ◆ **Practice:** When you are feeling overwhelmed or overworked, it's time to step away and play a game. It may be with family or friends or alone. Keep it simple and low tech. Cards or a variety of board games can not only be fun but also ensure that you and others stop spending so much time in isolation on your phones. Reflect on your downtime (on trips, after dinner, weekends, as a break, etc.) and how this might give you more enjoyable time together.
  - ◆ **Promise:** Gives you an enjoyable moment here and there to unwind and have old-fashioned fun.
- **Pre-set 14: Start the gratitude engine**
  - ◆ **Premise:** It's easy not only to get distracted but also to waste a lot of attention complaining. Thankfulness is a way to focus on what's essential.
  - ◆ **Practice:** During the day, note where your mind starts to criticize. This could occur while waiting in a restaurant, at home when you are impatient, or in a meeting where you are frustrated with others. Not only does complaining make us distracted, but it is also a huge energy drain. Notice how and when your mind starts trash talking and attempt to turn the negative energy into positive thoughts. Let your mind be grateful that you can afford a good meal, that you have healthy children, that you are gainfully employed. Turn that frown upside down!
  - ◆ **Promise:** Helps you notice that once you spend a few moments carefully thinking about the many things you are grateful for, your anxieties, worries, and complaints start to diminish.

- **Pre-set 15: The daily download**
  - ◆ **Premise:** Every day, people ask each other "What's new?" or "How was your day?" and then ignore what's said as soon as the other person starts talking. Active listening is completely absent.
  - ◆ **Practice:** The next time you ask someone about a project, their day, or what's going on, decide to actively listen to what they say. Ask better questions and be engaged. You may not feel like doing it, but make the willful choice to be interested. Don't try to listen to agree, comment, or correct, but listen to understand. Notice how much noise inside your own head prevents you from staying in the conversation. Give yourself 15 minutes of "present listening" as a gift in the moment.
  - ◆ **Promise:** Watch how these moments impact the quality of important connections and relationships.
- **Pre-set 16: DND: A sign of the times**
  - ◆ **Premise:** People will disturb you if they think they can—or if you don't notify them that they can't. Give them a basic way to know when it's okay to interrupt.
  - ◆ **Practice:** Make a small sign (or buy a pair of headphones) that clearly indicates that it's quiet time. A "do not disturb" warning like this might seem a bit drastic at first, but it tells people that you need to concentrate and that interruptions aren't welcome. This not only protects your time and attention but also sets a standard for others to see that your focus is precious and distractions are undesirable.
  - ◆ **Promise:** Creates a simple rule for people to follow that generates a balance between quiet and collaboration.
- **Pre-set 17: One-minute meeting set-up**
  - ◆ **Premise:** People love to grumble about how much they hate meetings because they're a huge waste of time. Yet nobody speaks up to stop the madness.

- ◆ **Practice:** Whether you're a meeting organizer or a participant, demand change. That means publishing formal agendas—prepared and distributed well in advance—is a requirement. By making them an essential way you work, you're ensuring you're not informally complicit in an agreement to waste everyone's precious time. You wouldn't write a book or perform a play without chapters and acts, yet every countless, meaningless meeting defaults to improv comedy as its model.

- ◆ **Promise:** Gets you all headed in the right direction with a simple agenda with clear objectives, roles, and expectations.

- **Pre-set 18: A few good friends**

  - ◆ **Premise:** Technology in any form—texting, social media, e-mail, podcasts, videoconferencing—can never supplant the sound of a close colleague's voice or the warmth of a friend's face.

  - ◆ **Practice:** Who are your best friends and closest contacts? That's a tough question for me and for most. Give it careful consideration. Know who these people are and keep in touch. The list might be short, so make it a point to stay in regular contact with them. Don't let either time or technology get between you and them.

  - ◆ **Promise:** Encourages you to make sure that you don't ever lose close, personal contact with people who really care about you. Much of the noise should die down when those people are around.

- **Pre-set 19: Set some automated rules and filters**

  - ◆ **Premise:** If you don't tell tech no, it will walk through the door uninvited every time. And the next time, it will invite all its friends.

  - ◆ **Practice:** Technology, in all of its forms and flavors, has no heart and no care or concern for you and your time. You need to use every tool at your disposal to prevent it from taking over your life. It starts with setting simple rules or filters, whether it is

directing e-mails to the trash or select folders or more sophisti-
cated schemes to manage alerts, notifications, and noises. What
starts as a small ping can quickly become a symphony of distractions and interruptions all disguised as an important guest,
surprisingly arriving at your doorstep without an invitation. Set
some guidelines that can handle their unexpected arrival.

+ **Promise:** Gets you ready in advance to field the constant
  influx of useless information and endless interruptions that
  weaken your focus and ruin your quality of life.

- **Pre-set 20: Soundproof spaces**

  + **Premise:** We need set-aside areas that restrict nonstop noise.
    Only with these silent refuges can we keep calm and carry on.

  + **Practice:** Find, design, and designate spaces in your life for
    silence. Whether this means a tech-free conference room or a
    small reading nook in your home, build and bless it as a safe
    haven. Go there frequently to regroup, think, meditate, con-
    template, pray, and plan. Make sure that technology isn't there
    or available nearby. Enjoy how silence restores and rejuvenates
    you from the constant clamor that is your world.

  + **Promise:** Provides time for reflection and wonder since silent
    spaces are what we crave when we are barraged by noise all day.

Click some of these pre-sets during your day. Make new ones that I
could never imagine. Share them and use them for your collective gain.

Personal Pre-set Programming: Customize Your Settings to Manage the Noise

Imagine you drive your car to a new city. When you turn on the
radio, your pre-sets no longer tune in to your favorite stations.
Instead, they only produce loud static. It's time to reset them to avoid
the noise. The same is true in your daily life; circumstances change
and you need to adapt.

I have created a programming guide that helps you personalize your pre-sets to accommodate your life circumstances. By following along, you can develop specific strategies to improve your focus. Take a notepad, sheet of paper, laptop, or device to answer these questions and develop your personal pre-set plan. Go to www.thebrieflab.com/tools to download a Personal Pre-set Programming Guide.

Step 1: Scan

You need to assess what's on the airwaves. Take some time to consider the impact of noise in your life. Then answer the following questions:

- *Risk Assessment:*
  - ◆ In three to five years, what could your professional and personal life look like if the noise has its way and takes control (worst-case scenario)? Write down a list of the top 10 possibilities.

- *Reward Assessment:*
  - ◆ In three to five years, what could your personal and professional life look like if you set effective boundaries on the noise in your life and environment (best-case scenario)? Write down a list of the top 10 possibilities.

Step 2: Identify AM (Attention Management) Stations

Considering your answers above, outline some practical priorities when it comes to managing your attention that will take you closer to your best-case scenario.

- List some changes you can make at work or home that will make it easier for you to be productive.
- List some ways you can limit distractions while you're trying to pay attention.
- List some ways you can limit time on screens or devices when you're not working.

Step 3: Identify FM (Focus Managers) Stations

- List concrete ways you can help your team, family, or friends to have more productive conversations and interactions.

- List ways you can encourage more efficient meetings or more productive social environments.

- List standards you can set and enforce for your business and personal interactions.

Step 4: Select Your Pre-sets

- Study the opportunities you have just outlined and chart them in a graph like the one below. Notice that some have a very high impact and will take longer to put into place, whereas others can be done quickly and make a big difference right away.

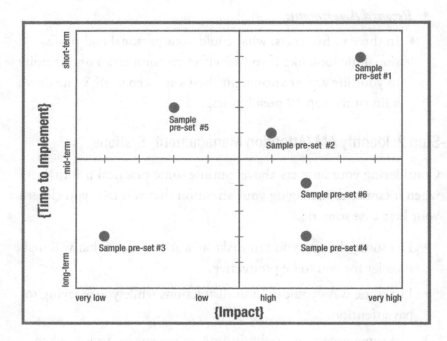

Now, select a few AM and FM tactics that can yield results and chart them out with their time to implement (short-term through long-term) and potential impact (very low through very high). Use the pre-sets as your guide, but don't limit your list to them.

Remember fewer and easier is better. Don't fall in love with your whole list—you won't make progress on 25 things. This will allow you to set up a plan to prioritize what you need to change over time. Mastering some quick changes will give you momentum to tackle the more difficult ones.

Step 5: Save and Share Your Pre-sets

If only we could convert these presets into lasting habits by simply pushing a button on the radio! But life isn't quite that easy. Instead, it will take practice, accountability, and discipline. But you can do it, one step at a time.

Write down your pre-sets and post them in a couple of places where you'll see them. Next, share them with someone you trust and ask them to hold you accountable every couple of weeks. Finally, review and update this document every 90 days as you make progress toward eliminating the static.

This will give you a practical way to gain greater focus and the strength to help others do the same.

"The Lineup": Playing to Win by Keeping Score

In sports, every coach needs a plan before each game. The list of who is going to play is generally called your lineup. It seems like an obvious thing, yet many games are lost because the wrong players are in, or missing from, the lineup.

I've devised a basic checklist for you to use to manage the day-to-day noise mindfully. Some of the actions are considered "daily" and others "specialty," with the distinction being that some actions are non-negotiable and must get scheduled in specific moments in time every day ("daily"), while others are ongoing, selective habits that can be plugged in strategically and selectively throughout the day ("specialty").

"Daily"—Scheduled behaviors

- **First thought:** This is your initial headline the moment you wake up and get out of bed. The thought sets the course for the day, helping you avoid the instinct to reach for your phone, start complaining, or let your mind grasp any random thought. Take time the night before to write down what you would like your silent statement to be.

- **Quiet time—a.m.:** Establish a set period in the morning, usually 15 minutes or more, dedicated to mindful reflection, contemplation, daydreaming, planning, thinking, silence, and/or prayer. It needs to be treated as a scheduled appointment for you and your thoughts and is non-negotiable, meaning it never gets canceled.

- **Read time:** Set aside exactly 10 minutes every day to read. Build a reading list and pick a book and read a little bit every day. It fuels the mind to focus on the things that matter in different parts of your life. You'll be amazed not only by how many books you can read in a year but also by how hard it is to stop when the 10 minutes are up.

- **Daily scan:** This is a brief moment during the day, about one to three minutes, to quickly reflect on your day ahead and to repair the one behind. It's essential to be mentally ready for what's coming toward you while also reviewing your past day. Determine the best time for you to do this, whether it is morning, mid-day or at night.

- **The big moment:** There is always one moment of the day that stands above the others. Given your specific roles in life, determine what that moment is and be ready to throw your mind and body into focusing on making that moment really matter. This moment may stay the same for a while or change day to day.

- **Quiet time—p.m.:** Establish a set period in the afternoon or evening, usually 15 minutes or more, dedicated to mindful reflection, contemplation, daydreaming, planning, thinking, silence, and/or prayer. It needs to be treated as a scheduled appointment for you and your thoughts and is non-negotiable, meaning it never gets canceled.

- **Final thought:** When you go to sleep, determine what your headline should be for the day. It is a definitive moment to conclude the day, no matter how it went. Checking your phone shouldn't be your last thought.

"Specialty"—Ongoing behaviors

- **Presence of mind:** Catch the thoughts that cross your mind during the day, whether willful, inspired, or accidental. It means keeping your head in the game by consistently asking yourself "What am I thinking about?" "What am I focusing on?" "Where's my mind?"

- **Rhythm of repetition:** Utilize an adage, quote, thought, mantra, or concern that is repeated inaudibly, yet purposefully, throughout the day. It helps you stay focused and centered on what's most important to you, given your role that day. Let yourself repeat it and don't worry about how many times you say it.

- **Mute more often:** Say "no" more often to the disruptions and distractions that are all around you. When you notice the noise start to build, use this to defeat it before it weakens you. No is a strong weapon, so choose to use it.

- **Take 5:** Set aside exactly five minutes to tackle a specific thought or task. Don't deceive yourself into thinking that you can successfully juggle many things at the same time. There are moments that demand intense concentration, so set the timer. When it's up, pause before proceeding.

- **Present listening:** Improve your quality of listening given to someone in the moment. Though it's hard sometimes, choose to pay closer attention to what's being said, without an agenda. It means listening not to respond, agree, fix, or solve, but to understand.

- **Brevity:** Practice clear and concise communication, both written and verbal. So much poor communication is the source of noise, so decide to become a lean communicator in moments that really matter. Brevity builds clarity.

This is a simple list, so live it. Live "the lineup" daily and see how your focus improves. You can go to www.thebrieflab.com/tools and find this tool (and others) in the resource section.

The noise definitely needs abatement, so make that your mission.

It's surely mine. No more noise.

{ The Lineup™ }

DAILY PLAYERS ► Role Details

DAILY PLAYER	NOTES
☐ First Thought Headline to start your day	
☐ Quiet Time—AM Moments just for your thoughts	
☐ Read Time Tackle your reading list	
☐ Daily Scan Looking ahead and behind	
☐ The Big Moment What matters most in the day	
☐ Quiet Time—PM Moments just for your thoughts	
☐ Final Thought Headline that wraps up your day	

DAILY PLAYERS are needed to compete every day.

Their planned presence and performance are essential to consistently defeat the noise day to day.

SPECIALTY PLAYERS ► Role Details

SPECIALTY PLAYER	NOTES
☐ Presence of Mind Thinking about your thinking	
☐ Rhythm of Repetition Using words & phrases to focus	
☐ Mute More Often Say no to devices & distractions	
☐ Take 5 Focus on one thing for 5 minutes	
☐ Present Listening The quality of your listening	
☐ Brevity Communicating clearly & concisely	
☐ Other Alternate ways to manage noise	

SPECIALTY PLAYERS give you options to adjust your ongoing game plan.

Their presence gives you unique ways to focus on winning moment to moment, day to day.

► Filling out { The Lineup™ } every day gives you a strong advantage to compete and defeat the noise.

22 That Sounds Wonderful

It might be easy to get discouraged while reading this book. When I talk to people about the impact of what's been previously discussed here, I often see their faces change and their moods drop. They may start looking at the future with a sense of hopelessness and frustration. It may seem dire. They start to wonder how current and future generations will be able to adapt and navigate such dramatic change. Will our youth even care to change their behavior or just give in to a divided mind and depleted focus as their reality?

We all might begin to ask some really tough questions:

- Will weapons of mass distraction permanently hurt how our children develop?
- How can we maintain healthy relationships and friendships when we consistently and habitually tune each other out?
- Will the art of listening and conversation be lost forever?
- Will we become more addicted to devices and grow more isolated from each other?
- Will screen time be something we strictly manage and struggle to avoid?

- Do the workplace, schools, and homes become places of productivity and fulfillment or endless sources of distraction and frustration?

- Will we lose our interest and ability to read long books, like the classics?

- Will e-mail and texting lead to new methods and applications that batter and drain the brain?

- Will virtual reality finally turn our heads into mush?

- Will civility be lost to shouting, closed-mindedness, and avoidance?

- How impersonal and shallow will we become before nobody cares anymore?

When we ponder these questions, it's really hard to be encouraged. How can we construct reasons for optimism?

The answer is in our strength to choose and fight for what's best for us, our friends, colleagues, and families. Although these social pressures may seem to inevitably force us to a darker, predetermined place, we can set our sights on how we want to manage this new reality, not have it manage us.

I wrote this book as an old-school response to a new-world problem. It's meant to give us practical means to adapt, discovering ways to live and lead when nobody can focus. It's meant to help us fight back against all the noise.

When I think about all of us confidently rising to the occasion, I think about my late brother, Johnny. He passed away in late 2015 after a long battle with cancer and hadn't yet turned 50 years old. He was an optimist, dearly loved people, and laughed a lot. He listened better than anyone I know and loved being in the moment.

It was a habit for him to focus on other people, and they felt it.

Johnny McCormack

That said, he also loved technology, television, and social media. He would post funny things and even follow celebrities online. He was a master at posting and texting the insightful, along with some inane comments, here and there.

But when you were with him, none of those things mattered—*you* counted most. He was a present listener, said no to the distractions, and created silence and quiet time for himself and those around him.

Johnny put people first. Especially during his last year with us, he helped others focus on the more important things in life. He attended to others before helping himself.

Time with him was precious because he put those around him first.

Since we were kids, when I was with him, there wasn't noise, just the beautiful sound of laughter, love, and life. I can still hear those wonderful sounds.

Let's be like Johnny.

RECOMMENDED READING

Allen, David. *Getting Things Done: The Art of Stress-Free Productivity*. New York: Little Brown Book Group, 2015.

Alter, Adam L. *Irresistible: The Rise of Addictive Technology and the Business of Keeping Us Hooked*. New York: Penguin Books, 2018.

Brewer, Judson, and Jon Kabat-Zinn. *The Craving Mind: From Cigarettes to Smartphones to Love—Why We Get Hooked & How We Can Break Bad Habits*. New Haven, CT: Yale University Press, 2017.

Cain, Susan. *Quiet: The Power of Introverts in a World That Can't Stop Talking*. New York: Crown Publishing Group, 2012.

Carr, Nicholas. *The Shallows: What the Internet Is Doing to Our Brains*. New York: W.W. Norton & Company, 2011.

Egan, Gerard, and Robert J. Reese. *The Skilled Helper: A Problem-Management and Opportunity-Development Approach to Helping*. Boston: Cengage, 2019.

George, Bill W., and Peter E. Sims. *True North: Discover Your Authentic Leadership*. Hoboken, NJ: John Wiley & Sons, 2007.

George, Bill. *Discover Your True North*. San Francisco: Jossey-Bass, 2007.

Goleman, Daniel. *Focus: The Hidden Driver of Excellence*. New York: Harper, 2015.

Grace, Annie. *This Naked Mind: Control Alcohol: Find Freedom, Rediscover Happiness & Change Your Life*. New York: Avery, an imprint of Penguin Random House, 2018.

Hammond, Claudia. *Time Warped: Unlocking the Mysteries of Time Perception*. New York: Harper Perennial, 2013.

Jampolis, Melina. *The Doctor on Demand Diet: Your Prescription for Lasting Weight Loss*. Los Angeles, CA: Ghost Mountain Books, 2015.

Kabat-Zinn, Jon. *Mindfulness for Beginners*. Mumbai: Jaico Publishing House, 2017.

Kahneman, Daniel. *Thinking, Fast and Slow*. New York: Farrar, Straus and Giroux, 2015.

Kethledge, Raymond Michael, and Michael S. Erwin. *Lead Yourself First: Inspiring Leadership through Solitude.* New York: Bloomsbury, 2019.

Kondō, Marie. *The Life-Changing Magic of Tidying Up: The Japanese Art of Decluttering and Organizing.* CreateSpace Independent Publishing Platform, 2016.

Macknik, Stephen L., and Susana Martinez-Conde. *Sleights of Mind: What the Neuroscience of Magic Reveals about Our Brains.* New York: Profile, 2012.

McKeown, Greg. *Essentialism: The Disciplined Pursuit of Less.* New York: Crown Business, 2014.

Medina, John. *Brain Rules: 32 Principles for Surviving and Thriving at Work, Home and School.* Seattle, WA: Pear Press, 2014.

Mello, Anthony De. *Awareness.* New York: Doubleday, 1990.

Newport, Cal. *Digital Minimalism: Choosing a Focused Life in a Noisy World.* New York: Portfolio/Penguin, 2019.

Pang, Alex Soojung-Kim. *Rest: Why You Get More Done When You Work Less.* New York: Penguin Life, 2018.

Pink, Daniel H. *A Whole New Mind: Why Right-Brainers Will Rule the Future.* New York: Riverhead Books, 2012.

Roberts, James A. *Too Much of a Good Thing: Are You Addicted to Your Smartphone?* Austin, TX: Sentia Publishing Company, 2016.

Schwartz, Barry. *The Paradox of Choice: Why More Is Less.* New York: Ecco Press, 2016.

Shafir, Rebecca Z. *The Zen of Listening: Mindful Communication in the Age of Distraction.* Wheaton, IL: Theosophical Publishing House, 2003.

Tan, Chade-Meng. *Search Inside Yourself: The Unexpected Path to Achieving Success, Happiness (and World Peace).* New York: HarperCollins, 2014.

Wilkinson, Michael. *The Secrets of Facilitation: The S.M.A.R.T. Guide to Getting Results with Groups.* San Francisco: Jossey-Bass, 2004.

Williams, James. *Stand out of Our Light: Freedom and Resistance in the Attention Economy.* Cambridge, UK: Cambridge University Press, 2018.

Wolf, Maryanne, and C. J. Stoodley. *Reader, Come Home: The Reading Brain in a Digital World.* New York: Harper, 2018.

Zomorodi, Manoush. *Bored and Brilliant: How Spacing Out Can Unlock Your Most Productive and Creative Self.* New York: Picador, 2018.

NOTES

Chapter 1: Noise, Noise, So Much Noise

1. Kevin Kelly, "In the Future You Will Own Nothing and Have Access to Everything," *Boing Boing,* July 14, 2016, boingboing.net/2016/07/14/in-the-future-you-will-own-not.html.

Chapter 2: Huh? We're Going Collectively Deaf

1. Geoffrey Chaucer, *Troilus and Criseyde* (SMK Books, 2018).

2. Carole Mahoney, "Why Don't We Trust Salespeople?" *Unbound Growth,* August 25, 2017, www.unboundgrowth.com/blog/why-dont-we-trust-salespeople.

Chapter 3: Brain Basics: Are Your Penguins Falling Off the Iceberg?

1. Christof Koch, "Does Brain Size Matter?" *Scientific American,* January 1, 2016, www.scientificamerican.com/article/does-brain-size-matter1/.

2. Bailey Johnson "Study: 3-Second Distractions Double Workplace Errors," CBS News, January 15, 2013, www.cbsnews.com/news/study-3-second-distractions-double-workplace-errors/.

3. Kristin Wong, "How Long It Takes to Get Back on Track After a Distraction," *Lifehacker,* Gizmodo, July 29, 2015, lifehacker.com/how-long-it-takes-to-get-back-on-track-after-a-distract-1720708353.

4. William C. Shiel, "Definition of Working Memory," *MedicineNet,* January 25, 2017, www.medicinenet.com/script/main/art.asp?articlekey=7143.

5. Daniel J. Levitin, *The Organized Mind: Thinking Straight in the Age of Information Overload* (New York: Dutton, 2016).

6. Will Knight, "'Info-Mania' Dents IQ More than Marijuana," *New Scientist,* April 22, 2005, www.newscientist.com/article/dn7298-info-mania-dents-iq-more-than-marijuana/.

7. Jon Hamilton, "Think You're Multitasking? Think Again," NPR, October 2, 2008, www.npr.org/templates/story/story.php?storyId=95256794.

8. Daniel J. Levitin, "Why the Modern World Is Bad for Your Brain," *The Guardian*, January 18, 2015, www.theguardian.com/science/2015/jan/18/modern-world-bad-for-brain-daniel-j-levitin-organized-mind-information-overload.

9. "Dopamine," *Psychology Today*, 2019, www.psychologytoday.com/us/basics/dopamine.

10. Steven Rosenbaum, "Digital Dopamine: When 'Delightful' Becomes a Drug," *HuffPost*, Verizon Media, October 30, 2017, www.huffpost.com/entry/digital-dopamine-when-delightful-becomes-a-drug_n_59f73a32e4b05f0ade1b58bc.

11. Hilarie Cash, Cosette D. Rae, Ann H. Steel, and Alexander Winkler, "Internet Addiction: A Brief Summary of Research and Practice," *Current Psychiatry Reviews* 8, no. 4 (2012): 292–298. doi:10.2174/157340012803520513.

12. Simon Parkin, "Has Dopamine Got Us Hooked on Tech?" *The Guardian*, March 4, 2018, www.theguardian.com/technology/2018/mar/04/has-dopamine-got-us-hooked-on-tech-facebook-apps-addiction.

13. Michael Winnick, "Putting a Finger on Our Phone Obsession," *Dscout*, June 16, 2016, blog.dscout.com/mobile-touches.

14. Ibid.

15. David Kelleher, "Survey: 81% of U.S. Employees Check Their Work Mail Outside Work Hours [INFOGRAPHIC]," *Tech Talk*, GFI Software, May 20, 2013, techtalk.gfi.com/survey-81-of-u-s-employees-check-their-work-mail-outside-work-hours/.

16. Joe McCormack, "BRIEF Survey," February 4, 2017.

Chapter 4: Living in an Info Junkie Crack House

1. Kiki McMillan, Kathie Flood, and Russ Glaeser, "Virtual Reality, Augmented Reality, Mixed Reality, and the Marine Conservation Movement," *Aquatic Conservation: Marine and Freshwater Ecosystems* 27, no. S1 (September 2017): 162–168. https://doi.org/10.1002/aqc.2820.

2. Sandee LaMotte. "The Very Real Health Dangers of Virtual Reality," CNN, December 13, 2017, www.cnn.com/2017/12/13/health/virtual-reality-vr-dangers-safety/index.html.

3. Ibid.

4. Ibid.

5. Biz Carson, "Mark Zuckerberg Has a Great Explanation for Why Virtual Reality Won't Be Isolating," *Business Insider,* February 28, 2016, www.businessinsider.com/mark-zuckerberg-on-vr-being-isolating-2016-2.

6. "New Approach Needed to Deliver on Technology's Potential in Schools," OECD, September 15, 2015, www.oecd.org/education/new-approach-needed-to-deliver-on-technologys-potential-in-schools.htm.

7. C. S. Lewis, *The Lion, the Witch, and the Wardrobe* (London: Geoffrey Bles, 1950).

Chapter 5: Always Stuck at School

1. Markham Heid, "We Need to Talk About Kids and Smartphones," *Time,* October 10, 2017, time.com/4974863/kids-smartphones-depression/.

2. Ibid.

3. Fiza Pirani, "What's Killing America's Teens? Inside CDC's New Mortality Report," *Atlanta Journal-Constitution,* June 1, 2018, www.ajc.com/news/national/what-killing-america-teens-inside-cdc-new-mortality-report/OeNlRXFCJqxZz5H7LsL5zJ/.

4. Heid, "We Need to Talk About Kids and Smartphones."

5. "Video Game Habit Change Summer Camp Ages 10 and Up," 2019, www.summerlandcamps.com/.

Chapter 7: The Loss of Civil Discourse

1. "Steve Leader Adams for Moore County Sheriff," 2018, adamsforsheriff.com/.

Chapter 8: Mind-Filled Momentum at Work

1. Thomas H. Kean and Lee Hamilton, *The 9/11 Commission Report* (National Commission on Terrorist Attacks upon the United States, 2004).

2. Ibid.

3. "September 11 Warning Signs Fast Facts," CNN, September 2, 2018, www.cnn.com/2013/07/27/us/september-11th-warning-signs-fast-facts/index.html.

4. Kean and Hamilton, *The 9/11 Commission Report.*

Chapter 10: Safety Briefing with Near Tragic Results

1. Patric McGroarty and Doug Cameron, "Southwest Accident Shows Passengers Unprepared for Emergencies," *Wall Street Journal*, April 19, 2018, www.wsj. com/articles/misused-masks-highlight-challenges-of-preparing-passengers-for-accidents-1524173260.

Chapter 11: Awareness Management 101

1. "How Many Emails Are Sent Every Day? And Other Top Email Statistics Your Business Needs to Know," *Templafy*, September 1, 2017, www.templafy.com/ blog/how-many-emails-are-sent-every-day-top-email-statistics-your-business-needs-to-know/.

2. Daniel Goleman, *Focus: The Hidden Driver of Excellence* (New York: Harper, 2015), 37–38.

3. "Udemy In Depth: 2018 Workplace Distraction Report," *Udemy Research*, 2019, research.udemy.com/research_report/udemy-depth-2018-workplace-distraction-report/.

4. Joe McCormack and Joseph Holtgrieve, "Engineering Mindfulness" (telephone interview), August 24, 2018.

5. Goldman, *Focus*.

Chapter 12: Take Aim: Set Your Sights on What Matters Most

1. Greg McKeown *Essentialism: The Disciplined Pursuit of Less* (New York: Crown Business, 2014).

2. Karl Bode "Ironically, Too Many Video Streaming Choices May Drive Users Back to Piracy," *Techdirt*, April 5, 2019, www.techdirt.com/ articles/ 20190320/07442041832/ironically-too-many-video-streaming-choices-may-drive-users-back-to-piracy.shtml.

3. Alina Tugend, "The Paralyzing Problem of Too Many Choices," *New York Times*, February 26, 2010, www.nytimes.com/2010/02/27/your-money/27shortcuts.html.

4. Joshua Becker, "21 Surprising Statistics That Reveal How Much Stuff We Actually Own," *Becoming Minimalist*, March 8, 2017, www.becomingminimalist.com/clutter-stats/.

5. Jon Kabat-Zinn, *Wherever You Go, There You Are* (London: Piatkus, 2004).

6. William Strunk and E. B. White, *The Elements of Style* (New York: Longman, 2000).

Chapter 13: Saying No to Noise

1. Judson Brewer, "Can Mindfulness Help You Quit Smoking?" NPR, June 24, 2016, www.npr.org/templates/transcript/transcript.php?storyId=483123383.

Chapter 14: Quiet Time: Restoring and Recharging Your Mind

1. Quiet, Please: Unleashing 'The Power of Introverts,'" NPR, January 30, 2012, www.npr.org/2012/01/30/145930229/quiet-please-unleashing-the-power-of-introverts.

2. Jory Heckman, "Despite Open Office Trend, Federal Employees Not Thrilled with Results," *Federal NewsNetwork*, September 25, 2018, federalnewsnetwork.com/workforce/2018/09/despite-open-office-trend-federal-employees-not-thrilled-with-results/.

3. Ethan S. Bernstein and Stephen Turban, "The Impact of the 'Open' Workspace on Human Collaboration," *Philosophical Transactions of the Royal Society B: Biological Sciences* 373, no. 1753 (August 19, 2018).

4. Dan Buettner, "Are Extroverts Happier Than Introverts?" *Psychology Today*, May 14, 2012, www.psychologytoday.com/us/blog/thrive/201205/are-extroverts-happier-introverts.

5. Daniel Goldman, *Focus: The Hidden Driver of Excellence* (New York: Harper, 2015), 56–57.

6. Ellie Polack, "New Cigna Study Reveals Loneliness at Epidemic Levels in America," *Cigna*, May 1, 2018, www.cigna.com/newsroom/news-releases/2018/new-cigna-study-reveals-loneliness-at-epidemic-levels-in-america.

7. Michael S. Erwin, *Lead Yourself First—Inspiring Leadership through Solitude* (London: Bloomsbury, 2017).

8. "Sleep Disorder Statistics—Research and Treatments," American Sleep Association, 2019, www.sleepassociation.org/about-sleep/sleep-statistics/.

9. Joe McCormack, "BRIEF Survey," February 4, 2017.

10. Meghan Rabbitt, "The Incredible Results You Get From Walking 30 Minutes A Day," *Yahoo!*, December 5, 2015, www.yahoo.com/lifestyle/the-incredible-results-you-get-1307743216025654.html.

11. Karen Murphy et al. *This Is Spinal Tap*. Santa Monica, CA: Metro Goldwyn Mayer Home Entertainment, 1984.

Chapter 16: Focus Management 101

1. "Media Usage in an Internet Minute as of June 2018," *Statista,* last edited May 8, 2018, www.statista.com/statistics/195140/new-user-generated-content-uploaded-by-users-per-minute/.

Chapter 17: Wanted: BRIEF Communicators

1. Jon Keegan, "Business Buzzwords Generator," *Wall Street Journal,* projects.wsj. com/buzzwords2014/#p=8%7C44%7C7%7C13%7C%7C%7C1.

2. Jim Edwards, "This Memo from Winston Churchill on 'Brevity' Is All You Need to Improve Your Writing," *Business Insider,* May 16, 2017, www. businessinsider.com/memo-winston-churchill-on-brevity-improve-writing-2017-5.

Chapter 18: Communicate Like a Magician

1. Ira Glass, "619: The Magic Show." *This American Life*, June 30, 2017.

2. Scott Simon and Susana Martinez-Conde, "The Science Behind Sleight Of Hand," NPR, August 9, 2008, www.npr.org/templates/story/story. php?storyId=93465269.

3. Glass, "619: The Magic Show."

4. Ibid.

Chapter 19: Preparing the Environment for Noise Abatement

1. "The Problem." Center for Humane Technology, humanetech.com/problem.

2. Kelsey Campbell-Dollaghan, "Here's the Final Nail in the Coffin of Open Plan Offices," *Fast Company,* July 19, 2018, www.fastcompany. com/90204593/heres-the-final-nail-in-the-coffin-of-open-plan-offices.

3. Susan Cullen, "6 Startling Statistics about Interruptions at Work," *NexaLearning,* February 21, 2011, www.nexalearning.com/blog/bid/50317/ 6-startling-statistics-about-interruptions-at-work.

4. Ben Renner, "Survey: Americans Spend Nearly Half Their Waking Hours Looking At Screens," *Study Finds,* January 15, 2019, www.studyfinds.org/ survey-americans-spend-half-waking-hours-looking-screens/.

5. Dave Chaffey, "How Many Connected Devices Do Consumers Use Today? #ChartOfTheDay," *Smart Insights,* August 3, 2016, www.smartinsights.com/traffic-building-strategy/integrated-marketing-communications/many-connected-devices-use-today-chartoftheday/.

6. Joshua Becker, "11 Reasons to Create a Technology-Free Bedroom," *Becoming Minimalist,* February 26, 2015, www.becomingminimalist.com/technology-free-bedroom/.

7. "What Impact Does the Environment Have on Us?" Regents of the University of Minnesota, 2016, www.takingcharge.csh.umn.edu/explore-healing-practices/healing-environment/what-impact-does-environment-have-us.

Chapter 20: Herding Cats: Facilitating to Focus More, Fidget Less

1. Dana Larsen, "Are Meetings Costing Your Business Too Much Money?" *Concur,* SAP, January 17, 2017, www.concur.com/newsroom/article/are-meetings-costing-your-business-too-much-money.

REFERENCES

"Steve Leader Adams for Moore County Sheriff," 2018, adamsforsheriff.com/.

Becker, Joshua. 2015. "11 Reasons to Create a Technology-Free Bedroom." *Becoming Minimalist*, February 26. www.becomingminimalist.com/technology-free-bedroom/.

Becker, Joshua. 2017. "21 Surprising Statistics That Reveal How Much Stuff We Actually Own." *Becoming Minimalist*, March 8. www.becomingminimalist.com/clutter-stats/.

Beyea, Suzanne. 2014. "Interruptions and Distractions in Health Care: Improved Safety With Mindfulness." *PS Net*, Agency for Healthcare Research and Quality, February, psnet.ahrq.gov/perspectives/perspective/152/interruptions-and-distractions-in-health-care-improved-safety-with-mindfulness.

Bode, Karl. 2019. "Ironically, Too Many Video Streaming Choices May Drive Users Back To Piracy." *Techdirt*, April 5. www.techdirt.com/articles/20190320/07442041832/ironically-too-many-video-streaming-choices-may-drive-users-back-to-piracy.shtml.

Brady, Ben. 2012. "WiFi Cold Spot." *Harvard Magazine*, June 19. www.youtube.com/watch?v=sg2–6RRa1E.

Brewer, Judson. 2016. "Can Mindfulness Help You Quit Smoking?" *NPR*, June 24. www.npr.org/templates/transcript/transcript.php?storyId=483123383.

Brooks, Mike. 2018. "How Much Screen Time Is Too Much?" *Psychology Today*, December 26. www.psychologytoday.com/us/blog/tech-happy-life/201812/how-much-screen-time-is-too-much.

Brownlee, John. 2009. "Study Says 64% of Men Don't Even Read the Manual before Calling Tech Support." *Geek.com*, November 9. www.geek.com/news/study-says-64-of-men-dont-even-read-the-manual-before-calling-tech-support-969371/.

Buettner, Dan. 2012. "Are Extroverts Happier Than Introverts?" *Psychology Today*, May 12. www.psychologytoday.com/us/blog/thrive/201205/are-extroverts-happier-introverts.

Campbell-Dollaghan, Kelsey. 2018. "Here Are Some Dread-Inducing Statistics on Open Plan Offices." *Fast Company*, November 14. www.fastcompany. com/90267251/here-are-some-dread-inducing-statistics-on-open-plan-offices.

Campbell-Dollaghan, Kelsey. 2018. "Here's the Final Nail in the Coffin of Open Plan Offices." *Fast Company*, July 19. www.fastcompany.com/90204593/ heres-the-final-nail-in-the-coffin-of-open-plan-offices.

Carson, Biz. 2016. "Mark Zuckerberg Has a Great Explanation for Why Virtual Reality Won't Be Isolating." *Business Insider*, February 28. www.businessinsider. com/mark-zuckerberg-on-vr-being-isolating-2016-2.

Chaffey, Dave. 2016. "How Many Connected Devices Do Consumers Use Today? #ChartOfTheDay." *Smart Insights*, August 3. www.smartinsights.com/traffic-building-strategy/integrated-marketing-communications/many-connected-devices-use-today-chartoftheday/.

Chaucer, Geoffrey. 2018. *Troilus and Criseyde*. SMK Books.

Cullen, Susan. 2011. "6 Startling Statistics about Interruptions at Work." *Nexa-Learning*, February 21. www.nexalearning.com/blog/bid/50317/6-startling-statistics-about-interruptions-at-work.

DiChristina, Mariette. 2012. "What Sleight Of Hand Reveals About Brain Function." *HuffPost*, May 17.

"Dopamine." 2019. *Psychology Today*. www.psychologytoday.com/us/basics/ dopamine.

Edwards, Jim. 2017. "This Memo from Winston Churchill on 'Brevity' Is All You Need to Improve Your Writing." *Business Insider*, May 26. www. businessinsider.com/memo-winston-churchill-on-brevity-improve-writing-2017-5.

Erwin, Michael S. 2017. *Lead Yourself First—Inspiring Leadership through Solitude*. New York: Bloomsbury, 2017.

"Experience on Demand: What Virtual Reality Is, How It Works, and What It Can Do." 2017. *Kirkus Reviews*, October 10. www.kirkusreviews.com/book-reviews/jeremy-bailenson/experience-on-demand/.

Farnell, Paul. 2017. "New Email Metrics: Two Seconds to Make an Impression." Litmus Software, Inc., March 9. litmus.com/blog/two-seconds.

Fox, Maggie, and Erika Edwards. 2019. "Teens Spend 'Astounding' Nine Hours a Day in Front of Screens: Researchers." West Virginia Education Association. www.wvea.org/content/teens-spend-astounding-nine-hours-day-front-screens-researchers.

Frost, Aja. 2016. "Only 3% of People Think Salespeople Possess This Crucial Character Trait." *HubSpot*, April 29. blog.hubspot.com/sales/salespeople-perception-problem.

Fruhlinger, Joshua. 2008. "95 Percent of All Returned Gadgets Still Work, Americans Don't Read Manuals." *Engadget*, June 3. www.engadget.com/2008/06/03/95-percent-of-all-returned-gadgets-still-work-americans-dont-r/.

"FuzeBox Survey Reveals U.S. Workforce Hampered by Multitasking and Disengagement." 2014. *Cision*, January 27. www.prnewswire.com/news-releases/fuzebox-survey-reveals-us-workforce-hampered-by-multitasking-and-disengagement-242217771.html.

Goleman, Daniel. 2015. *Focus: The Hidden Driver of Excellence*. New York: Harper, 37–38.

Hamilton, Jon. 2008. "Think You're Multitasking? Think Again." NPR, October 2. www.npr.org/templates/story/story.php?storyId=95256794.

Heckman, Jory. 2018. "Despite Open Office Trend, Federal Employees Not Thrilled with Results." *Federal News Network*, September 25. federalnewsnetwork.com/workforce/2018/09/despite-open-office-trend-federal-employees-not-thrilled-with-results/.

Heid, Markham. 2017. "We Need to Talk About Kids and Smartphones." *Time*, October 10. time.com/4974863/kids-smartphones-depression/.

"How Many Emails Are Sent Every Day? And Other Top Email Statistics Your Business Needs to Know." 2017. *Templafy*, September 1. www.templafy.com/blog/how-many-emails-are-sent-every-day-top-email-statistics-your-business-needs-to-know/.

"Internet & Tech Addiction Anonymous." *ITAA*, 2019, www.netaddictionanon.com/.

Jenkin, Matthew. 2015. "Tablets out, Imagination in: The Schools That Shun Technology." *The Guardian*, December 2. www.theguardian.com/teacher-network/2015/dec/02/schools-that-ban-tablets-traditional-education-silicon-valley-london.

Jiang, Jingjing. 2018. "How Teens and Parents Navigate Screen Time and Device Distractions." Pew Research Center, August 22. www.pewinternet.org/2018/08/22/how-teens-and-parents-navigate-screen-time-and-device-distractions/.

Johnson, Bailey. 2013. "Study: 3-Second Distractions Double Workplace Errors." CBS News, January 15. www.cbsnews.com/news/study-3-second-distractions-double-workplace-errors/.

Kabat-Zinn, Jon. 2004. *Wherever You Go, There You Are*. London: Piatkus.

Kean, Thomas H., and Lee Hamilton. 2004. *The 9/11 Commission Report*. National Commission on Terrorist Attacks upon the United States.

Keegan, Jon. n.d. "Business Buzzwords Generator." *Wall Street Journal*. projects.wsj.com/buzzwords2014/#p=8%7C44%7C7%7C13%7C%7C%7C1.

Keen, Andrew. 2018. "Can Virtual Reality Make Everything Better?" *The Washington Post*, March 2. www.washingtonpost.com/outlook/can-virtual-reality-make-everything-better/2018/03/02/911de440-1339-11e8-9065-e55346f6de81_story.html?noredirect=on&utm_term=.937993678a0e.

Kelleher, David. 2013. "Survey: 81% of U.S. Employees Check Their Work Mail Outside Work Hours [INFOGRAPHIC]." *Tech Talk*, GFI Software, May 20. techtalk.gfi.com/survey-81-of-u-s-employees-check-their-work-mail-outside-work-hours/.

Kelly, Kevin. 2016. "In the Future You Will Own Nothing and Have Access to Everything." *Boing Boing*, July 14. boingboing.net/2016/07/14/in-the-future-you-will-own-not.html.

Kim, Jungsoo, and Richard De Dear. 2013. "Workspace Satisfaction: The Privacy-Communication Trade-off in Open-Plan Offices." *Journal of Environmental Psychology* 36, 18–26. doi:10.1016/j.jenvp.2013.06.007.

Knight, Will. 2005. "'Info-Mania' Dents IQ More than Marijuana." *New Scientist*, April 22. www.newscientist.com/article/dn7298-info-mania-dents-iq-more-than-marijuana/.

Koch, Christof. 2016. "Does Brain Size Matter?" *Scientific American*, January 1. www.scientificamerican.com/article/does-brain-size-matter1/.

Lage, Ayana. 2017. "This Is How Many Americans Use Their Phones On The Toilet [Infographic]." *Daily Infographic*, November 5. www.dailyinfographic.com/how-many-americans-use-phones-on-toilet.

LaMotte, Sandee. 2017. "The Very Real Health Dangers of Virtual Reality." CNN, December 13. www.cnn.com/2017/12/13/health/virtual-reality-vr-dangers-safety/index.html.

Larsen, Dana. 2017. "Are Meetings Costing Your Business Too Much Money?" *Concur*, January 17. www.concur.com/newsroom/article/are-meetings-costing-your-business-too-much-money.

Levitin, Daniel J. 2016. *The Organized Mind: Thinking Straight in the Age of Information Overload*. New York: Dutton, 2016.

Levitin, Daniel J. 2015. "Why the Modern World Is Bad for Your Brain." *The Guardian*, January 18. www.theguardian.com/science/2015/jan/18/modern-world-bad-for-brain-daniel-j-levitin-organized-mind-information-overload.

Lewis, C. S. 1950. *The Lion, the Witch, and the Wardrobe*. London: Geoffrey Bles.

Magyari, Doug. 2016. "Virtual Reality: Are Health Risks Being Ignored?" CNBC, January 8. www.cnbc.com/2016/01/08/virtual-reality-are-health-risks-being-ignored-commentary.html.

Mahoney, Carole. 2017. "Why Don't We Trust Salespeople?" *Unbound Growth*, August 25. www.unboundgrowth.com/blog/why-dont-we-trust-salespeople.

McClinton, Dream. 2019. "Global Attention Span Is Narrowing and Trends Don't Last as Long, Study Reveals." *The Guardian*, April 17. www.theguardian.com/society/2019/apr/16/got-a-minute-global-attention-span-is-narrowing-study-reveals.

McCormack, Joe, and Joseph Holtgrieve. 2018. "Engineering Mindfulness." Telephone interview, August 24.

McCormack, Joe. 2017. "BRIEF Survey," February 4.

McCormack, Joe. 2017. *Tuning In, Tuning Out: Technology Is The New Noise*. The Brief Lab. thebrieflab.com/wp-content/uploads/2019/02/brief-report.pdf.

McGroarty, Patrick, and Doug Cameron. 2018. "Southwest Accident Shows Passengers Unprepared for Emergencies." *Wall Street Journal*, April 19. www.wsj.com/articles/misused-masks-highlight-challenges-of-preparing-passengers-for-accidents-1524173260.

McKeown, Greg. 2014. *Essentialism: the Disciplined Pursuit of Less*. New York: Crown Business.

"Media Usage in an Internet Minute as of June 2018." 2018. *Statista*, last edited May 8. www.statista.com/statistics/195140/new-user-generated-content-uploaded-by-users-per-minute/.

Molina, Brett. 2018. "Apple to Add 'Robust' Parental Tools to iPhones, iPads after Investors Warn of Addiction Risks." *USA Today*, January 9. www.usatoday.com/story/tech/news/2018/01/09/apple-add-robust-parental-tools-iphones-ipads-after-investors-warn-addiction-risks/1016571001/.

Morrison, Kyle W. 2013. "Distracted on the Job: Identifying and Minimizing Worker Distractions Can Help Reduce Injuries." *Safety+Health Magazine*, May 1. www.safetyandhealthmagazine.com/articles/distracted-on-the-job.

"New Approach Needed to Deliver on Technology's Potential in Schools." 2015. OECD, September 15. www.oecd.org/education/new-approach-needed-to-deliver-on-technologys-potential-in-schools.htm.

Nichols, Ralph G., and Leonard A. Stevens. 1957. "Listening to People." *Harvard Business Review*, Sept.ember. hbr.org/1957/09/listening-to-people.

Parkin, Simon. 2018. "Has Dopamine Got Us Hooked on Tech?" *The Guardian*, March 4. www.theguardian.com/technology/2018/mar/04/has-dopamine-got-us-hooked-on-tech-facebook-apps-addiction.

Pirani, Fiza. 2018. "What's Killing America's Teens? Inside CDC's New Mortality Report." *Atlanta Journal-Constitution*, June 1. www.ajc.com/news/national/what-killing-america-teens-inside-cdc-new-mortality-report/OeNlRXF-CJqxZz5H7LsL5zJ/.

Polack, Ellie. 2018. "New Cigna Study Reveals Loneliness at Epidemic Levels in America." Cigna, May 1. www.cigna.com/newsroom/news-releases/2018/new-cigna-study-reveals-loneliness-at-epidemic-levels-in-america.

Poole, Heather. 2015. "Dear Passengers: Safety on an Airplane Is No Joke." *Mashable*, October 14. mashable.com/2015/10/14/airplane-safety-is-serious/#xW4CWEpUq8qG.

Pritchard, Payton. 2019. "How Does RAM Work With the CPU?" Techwalla. www.techwalla.com/articles/how-does-ram-work-with-the-cpu.

"Quiet, Please: Unleashing 'The Power Of Introverts.'" 2012. NPR, January 30. www.npr.org/2012/01/30/145930229/quiet-please-unleashing-the-power-of-introverts.

Rabbitt, Meghan. 2015. "The Incredible Results You Get From Walking 30 Minutes A Day." Yahoo!, December 5. www.yahoo.com/lifestyle/the-incredible-results-you-get-1307743216025654.html.

Renee, Janet. 2019. "How Many Calories Does Celery Have?" *Healthfully*, January 10. healthfully.com/279493-how-many-calories-does-celery-have.html.

Renner, Ben. 2019. "Survey: Americans Spend Nearly Half Their Waking Hours Looking At Screens." Study Finds, January 15. www.studyfinds.org/survey-americans-spend-half-waking-hours-looking-screens/.

Rosenbaum, Steven. 2017. "Digital Dopamine: When 'Delightful' Becomes a Drug." *HuffPost*, October 30. www.huffpost.com/entry/digital-dopamine-when-delightful-becomes-a-drug_n_59f73a32e4b05f0ade1b58bc.

"September 11 Warning Signs Fast Facts." 2018. CNN, September 2. www.cnn.com/2013/07/27/us/september-11th-warning-signs-fast-facts/index.html.

Shaban, Hamza. 2018. "Study Links Restricting Screen Time for Kids to Higher Mental Performance." *The Washington Post*, September 27. www.washingtonpost.com/technology/2018/09/27/study-links-restricting-screen-time-kids-higher-mental-performance/?noredirect=on&utm_term=.7b43a0cd17c3.

Shiel, William C. 2017. "Definition of Working Memory." *MedicineNet*, January 25. www.medicinenet.com/script/main/art.asp?articlekey=7143.

Simon, Scott, and Susana Martinez-Conde. 2008. "The Science Behind Sleight Of Hand." NPR, August 9. www.npr.org/templates/story/story.php?storyId=93465269.

Sinha, R., et al. 2012. "Earthquake Disaster Simulation in Immersive 3D Environment," 15th World Conference on Earthquake Engineering 2012 (15WCEE): Lisbon, Portugal, September 24–28. www.iitk.ac.in/nicee/wcee/article/WCEE2012_3044.pdf.

"Sleep Statistics—Research & Treatments." *American Sleep Association*, 2019, www.sleepassociation.org/about-sleep/sleep-statistics/.

"Smartphone Addiction Creates Imbalance in Brain." 2017. Radiological Society of North America.

Smith, Aaron, and Monica Anderson. 2018. "Social Media Use in 2018." Pew Research Center, March 1. www.pewinternet.org/2018/03/01/social-media-use-in-2018/.

Strunk, William Jr. 2018. *Elements of Style*. SMK Books.

"The Problem." *Center for Humane Technology*, humanetech.com/problem.

Thibodeaux, Wanda. 2018. "Distractions Are Costing Companies Millions. Here's Why 66 Percent of Workers Won't Talk About It." *Inc.*, March 22. www.inc.com/wanda-thibodeaux/new-survey-shows-70-percent-of-workers-feel-distracted-heres-why.html.

Tschabitscher, Heinz. 2019. "The Number of Emails Sent Per Day in 2019 (and 20+ Other Email Facts)." *Lifewire*, January 3. www.lifewire.com/how-many-emails-are-sent-every-day-1171210.

Tucker, Ian, and Susan Cain. 2012. "Susan Cain: 'Society Has a Cultural Bias towards Extroverts.'" *The Guardian*, March 31. www.theguardian.com/technology/2012/apr/01/susan-cain-extrovert-introvert-interview.

Tugend, Alina. 2010. "The Paralyzing Problem of Too Many Choices." *New York Times*, February 26. www.nytimes.com/2010/02/27/your-money/27shortcuts.html.

Turner, Giles. 2018. "How Smartphones and Social Media Can Steal Childhood." *Bloomberg Businessweek*, May 3. www.bloomberg.com/news/articles/ 2018-05-04/how-smartphones-social-media-disrupt-childhood-quicktake.

Twenge, Jean M. 2018. *iGen: Why Today's Super-Connected Kids Are Growing up Less Rebellious, More Tolerant, Less Happy—and Completely Unprepared for Adulthood*: *and What That Means for the Rest of Us*. Atria International.

"Udemy In Depth: 2018 Workplace Distraction Report." 2019. Udemy Research. research.udemy.com/research_report/udemy-depth-2018-workplace-distraction-report/.

"Video Game Habit Change Summer Camp Ages 10 and Up." 2019. www. summerlandcamps.com/.

"Warren Buffett's 5-Step Process for Prioritizing True Success (and Why Most People Never Do It)." 2017. *Live Your Legend*, February 1. liveyourlegend.net/ warren-buffetts-5-step-process-for-prioritizing-true-success-and-why-most-people-never-do-it/.

"What Impact Does the Environment Have on Us?" 2016. Regents of the University of Minnesota. www.takingcharge.csh.umn.edu/explore-healing-practices/ healing-environment/what-impact-does-environment-have-us.

"Why Do We Say It Goes in One Ear and out the Other?" *BookBrowse.com*, www. bookbrowse.com/expressions/detail/index.cfm/expression_number/482/it-goes-in-one-ear-and-out-the-other.

Winnick, Michael. 2016. "Putting a Finger on Our Phone Obsession." *Dscout*, June 16. blog.dscout.com/mobile-touches.

Winston, George. 2017. "Simplicity—General Montgomery's Battle Plan for D-Day Was Hand-Written On One Page." *War History Online*, July 1. www. warhistoryonline.com/world-war-ii/battle-plans-d-day-released-m.html.

Wong, Kristin. 2015. "How Long It Takes to Get Back on Track After a Distraction." *Lifehacker*, July 29. lifehacker.com/how-long-it-takes-to-get-back-on-track-after-a-distract-1720708353.

Wong, Raymond. 2019. "There Are Officially Too Many Damn Video Streaming Services." *Mashable*, April 12. mashable.com/article/streaming-video-service-fatigue-netflix-disney-plus-apple-tv/.

ABOUT THE AUTHOR

Joe McCormack is passionate about helping people gain clarity when there is so much competing for our attention. In a world of shrinking attention spans and information overload, people struggle to focus.

An experienced marketing executive, successful entrepreneur, and author, Joe is recognized for his work in concise, strategic communication and leadership development. His book *BRIEF: Make a bigger impact by saying less* (John Wiley & Sons, 2014) tackles the timeliness of the less-is-more mandate. His new book, *NOISE: Living and leading when nobody can focus* (John Wiley & Sons, 2019) continues this conversation and addresses the daunting challenge of how to focus when the brain is bombarded by external and internal noise and unable to tune in.

An energetic leader, Joe founded The BRIEF Lab in 2013 after years dedicated to developing and delivering a unique curriculum on executive communication for US Army Special Operations Command (Fort Bragg, North Carolina). He actively counsels military leaders and senior executives on effective, efficient communication and produces the weekly podcast series *Just Saying*. The BRIEF Lab's mission is to help organizations create an elite standard of communication to improve operational efficiency and effectiveness.

Joe's clients include Mastercard, Grainger, Boeing, Harley-Davidson, TransUnion, BMO Harris Bank, DuPont, and a variety of US military units.

Previously, Joe served as SVP, Corporate Marketing at Ketchum, a top-five marketing agency in Chicago, where he directed its corporate marketing practice and introduced new service models to enhance messaging and deepen relationships with market influencers.

He received a BA in English literature from Loyola University of Chicago, where he graduated with honors. Joe is fluent in Spanish and has broad international experience.

Joe lives in suburban Chicago and Pinehurst, North Carolina.

ABOUT THE BRIEF LAB

People today are buried in information, constantly distracted, and frequently interrupted. They expect those around them to be brief and often get frustrated when they're not. When professionals are clear, concise, and compelling, they make people who are inundated feel an immediate sense of relief—less noise, more clarity.

The BRIEF Lab helps teams and organizations communicate more clearly and concisely when they need to make an impact. We challenge professionals to embrace that less is more; they need to recognize and adhere to an elite communication standard in a variety of difficult moments such as meetings, e-mails, updates, conversations, pitches, and presentations to secure deeper understanding and achieve a competitive advantage.

Clients at The BRIEF Lab range from elite military units and Fortune 1000 companies to progressive organizations that choose to invest in their leaders and teams to become more efficient and effective. They make a strong commitment to be lean communicators.

We offer a robust curriculum—including in-person workshops and online webinars—at our offices in suburban Chicago and Southern Pines, North Carolina, or offsite at client locations, where we teach leaders and teams to communicate clearly, succinctly, and effectively. What's more, we offer keynotes and webinars to inspire people to take action. Anyone in a leadership role—or anyone who aspires to one—can benefit from learning the BRIEF methodology and putting it into practice in a variety of circumstances. Leaders count on us to help their teams and organizations create a culture of brevity by mastering brevity. When they master the discipline to embrace lean communication, they save time, make faster and better decisions, develop stronger consensus, and improve operational performance.

The BRIEF Lab evolved from the Sheffield Company, a marketing agency founded by Joe McCormack in 2006, that specialized in narrative messaging and visual storytelling. In 2011, Joe was invited to develop a unique curriculum for US Army Special Operations Command (USASOC) at Fort Bragg, North Carolina, to teach special operators and staff personnel how to communicate with passion and precision. In early 2013, Joe wrote a book, *BRIEF: Make a bigger impact by saying less*, that set the stage for The BRIEF Lab to teach professionals the value of brevity.

Today, The BRIEF Lab's distinctive curriculum and coursework sets a high-level communication standard for leaders and teams to confidently communicate with greater confidence and achieve noticeable results wherever they operate.

More information can be found at www.thebrieflab.com.

INDEX